NATURALLY
NOURISHED

NATURALLY
healthy, delicious meals made
with everyday ingredients

NOURISHED

 My New Roots SARAH BRITTON

jacqui
small

Quarto is the authority on a wide range of topics.
Quarto educates, entertains and enriches the lives of
our readers – enthusiasts and lovers of hands-on living.
www.QuartoKnows.com

A catalogue record for this book is available
from the British Library.

Book and cover design by La Tricia Watford

Front cover and interior photography by
Sarah Britton

ISBN: 978 1 911127 35 2

This edition published in 2017 by

Jacqui Small LLP
74-77 White Lion Street
London N1 9PF

Copyright © 2017 by Sarah Britton

This edition published by arrangement with
Clarkson Potter/Publishers, an imprint of
the Crown Publishing Group, a division of
Penguin Random House LLC

2019 2018 2017

10 9 8 7 6 5 4 3 2 1

Printed in China

MIX
Paper from
responsible sources
FSC® C104723

To Mikkel and Finn, for the everlasting exchange of nourishment

CONTENTS

———

INTRODUCTION

———

It was just a head of cabbage sitting on my chopping board – humble, unassuming and quiet, not sexy like a strawberry. Not proud and convincing like broccoli, nor dignified or elegant like a carrot. Yet it was inexpensive, a staunch staple in my supermarket, and I wanted to make it shine. Play with it. Do *something* interesting with that lowly head or I would lose all faith that simple, common vegetables could be transformed to be something truly special. That I don't have to go to the farmers' market to create an inspired meal. And that I wouldn't have to slave over the hob to get dinner on the table.

I sliced the cabbage head into quarters, heated some vegetable stock, simmered the wedges, then set them in a searing-hot pan to char. That modest brassica was completely transformed into something so delicious that I could hardly contain my excitement. It was smoky and savoury and rich. I whipped together a sauce with toasted walnuts and garlic, added some chopped apple and parsley and quite suddenly I had created a meal with intense and complex flavours from such simple ingredients that it felt like the culinary triumph of my life.

After receiving yet another letter from a student asking me how she can eat healthily on her limited food budget and crazy work schedule, I considered the cabbage dish I had made the night before and realized *that* was the answer. Yes, I get jazzed about exotic ingredients, but really, the bulk of my diet consists of vegetables, fruit, legumes and grains that don't need a lot of doctoring up. In fact, most of my favourite ingredients are found at my neighbourhood supermarket. Those letters inspired me to create recipes that everybody can cook from, on almost any budget, any day of the week. Those letters inspired me to write this book.

We all know the importance of eating balanced, nourishing foods, but for many of us, the challenge of creating a healthy dinner can feel overwhelming when we think we have to make special trips to upscale grocers or health food stores for expensive ingredients, buy produce we can't use up and cook with techniques we may not be familiar with – on top of our day-to-day responsibilities. In fact, hyping up dinner to be a fancy affair can have the opposite intended effect: we can set ourselves up for failure. I want to help you overcome these challenges by giving you the building blocks for creating easy, delicious meals with basic storecupboard ingredients and affordable produce, using simple-to-master cooking skills. With time I hope you will gain enough confidence to riff on these recipes and make your own meals – and get excited about being creative in the kitchen.

This collection of recipes celebrates all the simple and good ingredients that you probably have in your fridge or that you can get right around the corner. If you are lucky enough to live near a nice supermarket, health food store or farmers' market, you're sure to find even more organic, local produce and inspiration there.

What writing this book has taught me is that healthy, delicious food doesn't have to be expensive or complicated. I have pushed, learned and high-fived myself more times during its creation than ever before, because up against the challenge, I have proved that we can eat well, even on a budget, even on a Tuesday.

INSPIRED WEEKNIGHT RECIPES

The book is laid out in five chapters loosely following the seasons – each chapter starting with spring and flowing through the year – but you can make these recipes all year round with produce available to you.

The first two chapters feature Satisfying Soups and Sumptuous Salads. Although the recipes in these chapters can be served as side dishes, all of them are filling enough to be the centrepiece of a busy weeknight meal.

You'll notice that most recipes include a 'Rollover' note. This shows you how one recipe rolls into another with leftover elements and will give you ideas on how to cook a bit more of one element (for example, chickpeas) to get a head start on another recipe in the book. This makes tomorrow's meal a whole lot easier: when using rollovers, you can easily plan your week of meals and groceries and save a lot of time. Rollovers are explained in more detail on page 11.

The Nourishing Mains chapter is full of unique and surprising ideas on how to transform supermarket basics into exciting main dishes. Although these recipes aren't complicated, they have a few more ingredients than the recipes in the other chapters. This is where the 'Rollover' boxes become especially handy, because they will prompt you to cook enough of one ingredient to make two meals.

The next chapter is Simple Sides and Small Plates. These dishes contain few ingredients and come together quickly, but will surprise you with their big, bold flavours. Each recipe can easily be turned into a main dish simply by using the ideas in the 'Sides Me Up!' box. If you're just starting out with healthy cooking, this is in fact a great chapter to begin with, as the recipes are fast and easy. The Sides and Small Plates are meant to accompany main dishes, or you can make several of them together to create a family-style spread.

Savoury and Sweet Snacks round out the book with little nibbles perfect for the four-o'clock munchies. Dips, spreads, crackers and the like also make fantastic starters, and combining them creates an impressive spread for special occasions. The healthy, sweet snacks are perfect for all-day enjoyment from breakfast to dessert, and many of them are portable, so they make luxurious lunchbox stuffers!

Each chapter opens with '3 Ways': a recipe with a simple base that you can easily change – everything from kale salad to chocolate brownie bites. Have fun with this one, and once you get the momentum going, create '3 Ways' of your very own. Also, the recipes are appropriately labelled with symbols so you can easily plan your meals: 'V' for vegan, 'GF' for gluten-free, 'R' for raw and 'GrF' for grain-free.

SIMPLIFY LIFE
IN THE KITCHEN

———

There are so many wonderful ways to save time in the kitchen, and even if you love to cook as much as I do, I'm sure you also love spending your precious hours doing other things as well.

BUILDING BLOCKS FOR EVERY MEAL

I approach cooking by looking at ingredients as building blocks. First, I create the foundation of the meal, which can be anything from grains to legumes, a vegetable or leafy greens. Once I have this in place, I add other elements to make the dish interesting, such as roasted veggies, avocado, hummus or even a soft-boiled egg. I can actually stop at this point if I don't have any more time, and I end up with a simple yet delicious little meal. If I do have more time, however, I'll make it special by adding some sprouts, salsa and/or goat's cheese, followed by a sauce or dressing. If I'm feeling really ambitious, I'll toast up some seeds, finely chop some herbs or chop fresh chillies to give the meal some flair.

Building blocks allow you to compose a dish based on an understanding of what it takes to make a delicious meal, instead of getting hung up on specific ingredients. Using this approach also enables you to identify the roles of the various ingredients in a specific

dish so you can easily adjust and customize them depending on what you already have in your fridge or storecupboard, what season it is, dietary preferences and tastes. You can even change old favourite recipes just by swapping out building blocks to create something totally new. Cooking becomes much more convenient, creative, free and fun!

An example of this approach is one dish that I eat very often for dinner: salads. Simply build your meal.

BUILD A FOUNDATION	MAKE IT INTERESTING	ADD SOMETHING SPECIAL	SAUCE IT UP (optional)	GIVE IT SOME FLAIR (optional)
quinoa	carrots	green lentils	Minty Tahini Dressing (page 63)	Dukkah (page 26)
brown rice	sweet potato	chickpeas	Romesco Sauce (page 195)	coriander
massaged kale	black lentils	soft-boiled egg	Chermoula (page 148)	crushed chilli flakes
wholegrain noodles or pasta	broccoli	mung bean sprouts (see Basic Sprouts, page 23)	Almond Butter Sauce (page 135)	Sesame Salt (page 157)
couscous	avocado	black beans	Radish Coriander Salsa (page 108)	toasted pumpkin seeds
whole roasted sweet potato	black beans	Spicy Lime Slaw (page 99)	Spicy Tahini Ginger Sauce (page 104)	toasted pecans
polenta	roasted beetroot	goat's cheese	Lemon-mint Date Sauce (page 57)	Ginger-pickled Carrots (page 87)
wholegrain bread	Basic Hummus (page 187) or other bean spread	lentil sprouts (see Basic Sprouts, page 23)	Rocket Pesto (page 141)	chopped olives

ROLLOVERS (COOKING MORE ON PURPOSE)

I've come up with a way to eat well every day without spending much time cooking at all, using what I call *rollovers*. A rollover is an intentional leftover that rolls right on into the next day, or even weeks.

For example, on Monday I cook quinoa for a big quinoa salad (see page 91), but I'll make double so that I have a rollover for Tuesday. Tuesday I'll cook double the lentils that I need for a quinoa and lentil dish, and I'll use the extra lentils for a Wednesday rollover. Wednesday I'll cook a big pot of brown rice to mix with the lentils, and so on.

Rollovers not only work with basic staples, but also with things like roasted vegetables, pastry, quick pickles, nut butter, seed cheese, toppings, dressing and sauces. You will in fact see examples of this in almost every recipe in the book. If you can spend more of your kitchen time 'assembling' rather than standing over a hot hob, cooking becomes a lot more fun and playful. Yes, there will be investment days when you'll make a big batch of granola bars, salad dressing and

brown rice, but then you'll have building blocks for many meals. You'll see your fridge and storecupboard filling up with these building blocks, and your meals will become faster to assemble, more balanced and delicious, while your time in the kitchen lessens.

USE YOUR FREEZER (NOT JUST FOR ICE CUBES!)

For many years my freezer was a storage space for ice lollies and long-forgotten hunks of bread. Then I realized that it could be so much more. . . it's like a food time machine! Freezing cooked foods, especially beans and grains, is a perfectly respectable way to stretch your time and meals.

Here are a few things I always have on hand in my freezer and how long they can keep for:

- **cooked beans (6 months)**
- **cooked grains (6 months)**
- **frozen vegetables, like green peas (8–10 months)**
- **bread, wraps, muffins, other baked goods (6 months)**

HOW TO BOOST FLAVOUR

Over many years of cooking, I've learned how to boost flavour in all kinds of food without the use of fancy equipment. The recipes in this book use all my favourite techniques, but I thought it would be fun to highlight them here to get you out of a cooking rut and get your own creative culinary juices flowing.

Grill and Char

If there is one technique to master it is this one. Grilling and charring food makes it delicious because of something called the Maillard Reaction. This complex process happens when sugars and amino acids in the food react to a high heat, creating and releasing hundreds of potent molecules that enhance the taste of what you are eating. Sounds complicated, but all you need to do is turn up the heat and get cooking! Remember that what you're after is caramelization, not burnt food. A fine line, but an important one.

TRY IT: Charred Aubergine Baba Ganoush with Pine Nuts (page 167), Grilled Caesar Salad with Chickpea Croûtons (page 61)

Toast

In line with grilling and charring, toasting also creates the Maillard Reaction, giving us the same food with a more intense flavour. The foods that benefit the most from toasting are nuts, seeds, spices, grains and of course bread. You can toast almost anything in a pan, but the slower and most effective way is actually in the oven. With odd-shaped ingredients like walnuts, a pan is only going to deliver heat to the parts of the food that it touches, usually creating burnt spots while the rest of the ingredient remains raw. In the oven you can surround the food with heat, creating an evenly toasted product that tastes really amazing. The only drawback with the oven is that you can't keep an eye on the food, so take the pan out of the oven often to prevent burning.

TRY IT: Toasted Walnut Sauce (page 84), Honey Almond Granola Bars (page 218)

Roast

A tried-and-true cooking method, this is one I use a *lot*. And not just for vegetables – fruit and cheese get the lovin' oven treatment too. The process of roasting helps the liquid to evaporate in the food you're cooking, which in turn intensifies the natural flavours. Sugars caramelize and sharp tastes mellow into something sweeter and more palatable.

TRY IT: Roasted Radishes and Avocado with Sesame Salt (page 157), Balsamic-roasted Plums with Spinach and Goat's Cheese (page 70)

Marinate or Infuse

This technique relies on an intensely flavoured combination of spices, herbs and seasoning to bathe your food in. This infuses the food with major taste. You can cook the food afterwards or leave it raw. Sometimes I recommend placing the food in the marinade after cooking, while it is still warm, which helps the food absorb even more flavour.

TRY IT: Marinated Roasted Red Peppers with Chickpeas (page 164), Portobello Pizzas (page 119)

Seasoning with Salt

Sometimes an extra pinch of salt can mean the difference between a plain dish and a really yummy one. If you feel like something is missing, try adding a little salt first and see if it makes a difference – especially in sweet foods and desserts (trust me on this). Salt your food in small increments as you cook, tasting as you go. My recipes tend to be less salty than what most people are used to, so you can salt food to suit your preference.

TRY IT: Broccoli with Garlic Ghee and Pine Nuts (page 171), Brilliant Banana Almond Soft-serve (page 221)

Add a Little Acid

If you ask most professional chefs what is missing in home-cooked meals, they will almost always say 'acid'. Acidity gives food sourness, brightness and tang, but most importantly, balance! There are two ways to add acidity to food: citrus (lemon or lime juice) or vinegar (I love apple cider vinegar). Pickles are a fabulous complement to many dishes, and it doesn't require much acidity to take your food from flat to fab; if you ever go overboard with the acid, add something sugary (for example, pure maple syrup) or fatty (for example, cold-pressed olive oil) to even things out.

TRY IT: Lemony Raw Beetroot and Quinoa Salad with Dill and Olives (page 91), Pico de Gallo (page 112)

Finish with Fat

Fat tastes good. In fact we are biologically hardwired to like the taste of fat because it is the densest form of energy out there, and for a long time our survival depended on it. Fat also helps us to feel satisfied – and thus it's an important aspect in any dish. We feel fuller longer by eating fats and oils because they take longer to digest, which is one reason that low-fat diets often fail – people tend to feel hungry soon after consuming low-fat foods. Because fruits and vegetables are relatively low in fat, most of my recipes are too. So I will often suggest drizzling the finished dish with olive oil, which not only delivers richness and creamy texture, but satiety as well.

TRY IT: Divine and Foolproof Mayonnaise (page 111), Brown Butter Carrots with Pistachios and Dill (page 163)

Garnish Before Serving

Adding edibles with tons of taste as you are finishing up the preparation and cooking is not really a technique, but it's an important way to increase the personality in foods. It's what will prompt your friends to exclaim, 'Wow! How did you make this?' and make you feel like a pro. Some of my favourite garnishes are fresh herbs, capers, olives, chilli flakes, citrus zest, toasted nuts and seeds, toasted coconut, spice blends, infused oil and nori flakes. Having one or more of these elements in your kitchen at all times gives you flavour superpowers.

TRY IT: So-simple Roasted Roots with Dukkah (page 183), Sesame Salt (page 157)

satisfying
SOUPS

PREVIOUS PAGE, from left to right: Spring Minestrone, page 17 / Summer Minestrone, page 18 /
Autumn Minestrone, page 19

MINESTRONE, 3 WAYS

Minestrone is a classic, fully-loaded Italian vegetable soup. Since it is typically made with seasonal ingredients, I took liberties and created three recipes – one each for spring, summer and autumn. Each of these soups tastes remarkably different, but all begin with oil, onion, salt and garlic, then veer off to wherever the season wills it. I love adding beans to give the soups more body and satiety, but lentils would also work well. If you do not want to add pasta to your soup, try using a julienne peeler to make noodles out of seasonal veggies, as I do in the summer version. *Buon appetito!*

SPRING MINESTRONE

SERVES 6–8 ——————————————————

1 Fill a medium saucepan with water and bring to the boil. Add 1½ teaspoons of the sea salt and the pasta, and cook until al dente, according to the instructions on the packet. Drain and set aside.

2 In a large stockpot or saucepan, melt the coconut oil over a medium heat. Add the yellow onions and remaining 1½ tablespoons of salt and stir to coat. Cook, stirring occasionally, until the onions soften and begin to slightly caramelize, about 10 minutes.

3 Add the garlic, spring onions and stock, and bring to the boil. Add the green peas, asparagus, mangetout and butter beans, and cook for 3–4 minutes until the peas are bright green.

4 Remove from the heat, add the Swiss chard, parsley, black pepper and lemon juice. Stir to wilt the chard.

5 Add the cooked pasta immediately before serving. Season with salt. Serve hot with a drizzle of cold-pressed olive oil.

2 tbsp fine sea salt

100 g / 3½ oz dried gluten-free or wholegrain shell pasta of your choice

1 tbsp coconut oil or ghee

3 medium yellow onions, diced

3 garlic cloves, finely chopped

4 spring onions, white and green parts, sliced

1.7 litres / 3 pints vegetable stock

150 g / 5½ oz green peas, fresh or frozen

225 g / 8 oz asparagus, chopped

100 g / 3½ oz mangetout, chopped

225 g / 8 oz (1 240 g / 8½ oz can) cooked butter beans, drained and rinsed

150 g / 5½ oz Swiss chard, chopped

15 g / ½ oz chopped fresh flat-leaf parsley

1 tsp freshly ground black pepper

1 tbsp freshly squeezed lemon juice

Cold-pressed olive oil, to serve

1 tbsp coconut oil or ghee

3 medium yellow onions, diced

1 tsp fine sea salt

3 garlic cloves, finely chopped

4 celery sticks, diced

1 red pepper (stem, seeds and ribs removed), diced

100 g / 3½ oz green beans, chopped

500 g / 1 lb 2 oz tomatoes, diced

1.5 litres / 2½ pints vegetable stock

225 g / 8 oz (1 240 g / 8½ oz can) cooked chickpeas, drained and rinsed

1 small courgette, sliced with a julienne peeler or spiralizer into long, thin strips, like spaghetti

7 g / ¼ oz fresh basil leaves

1 tsp freshly ground black pepper

Cold-pressed olive oil, to serve

SUMMER MINESTRONE

SERVES 6–8

1 In a large stockpot or pan, melt the coconut oil over a medium heat. Add the onions and salt and stir to coat. Cook, stirring occasionally, for about 10 minutes until the onions soften and begin to slightly caramelize.

2 Add the garlic, celery, pepper, green beans and tomatoes. Stir to coat and cook for about 5 minutes until fragrant.

3 Add the stock, bring to the boil, then reduce the heat to low and simmer for about 10 minutes until the vegetables are tender.

4 Remove from the heat and add the chickpeas, courgette and basil. Season with black pepper and serve with a drizzle of olive oil.

AUTUMN MINESTRONE

1 Fill a medium saucepan with water and bring to the boil. Add 1½ teaspoons of the sea salt and the pasta and cook according to the packet instructions until al dente. Drain and set aside.

2 In a large stockpot or saucepan, melt the coconut oil over a medium heat. Add the onions and remaining 1½ tablespoons of salt and stir to coat. Cook, stirring occasionally, for about 10 minutes until the onions soften and begin to slightly caramelize.

3 Add the garlic, rosemary, thyme, leeks, pumpkin and carrots. Stir to coat and cook for about 5 minutes until the herbs are fragrant.

4 Add the stock, bring to the boil, then reduce the heat to low and simmer for about 20 minutes until the pumpkin and carrots are tender.

5 Remove from the heat and add the kidney beans, spinach, black pepper and cooked pasta. Serve hot with a drizzle of olive oil.

2 tbsp fine sea salt

100 g / 3½ oz dried gluten-free or wholegrain corkscrew pasta of your choice

1 tbsp coconut oil or ghee

3 medium red onions, diced

3 garlic cloves, finely chopped

2 tbsp chopped fresh rosemary

1 tbsp fresh thyme leaves

3 leeks, white and light-green parts, chopped

400 g / 14 oz chopped pumpkin

5 medium carrots, chopped

2 litres / 3½ pints vegetable stock

250 g / 9 oz (1 400 g / 14 oz can) cooked kidney beans, drained and rinsed

60 g / 2¼ oz spinach or kale

1 tsp freshly ground black pepper

Cold-pressed olive oil, to serve

STORECUPBOARD PEA AND DILL SOUP

When I was in school studying holistic nutrition, I had so little time to cook and eat healthily that my studies versus my habits became a bit of a joke – but not one that I was laughing at! To remedy my feelings of utter hypocrisy, I came up with this wholesome and quick-to-make soup to power me through all-night study sessions. It continues to be one of my favourite meals, because I can keep all of the ingredients on hand, since the recipe uses frozen peas and dried dill. You can of course use fresh in both cases, but for anyone with a busy lifestyle, this is the ultimate convenience food. Even today, my Storecupboard Pea and Dill Soup usually ends up as dinner when there is 'nothing to eat' in the house.

SERVES 4 ————————

Knob of coconut oil or ghee

2 medium yellow onions

Fine sea salt

3 garlic cloves

500 g / 1 lb 2 oz frozen green peas

750 ml / 1¼ pints hot vegetable stock

1 tbsp dried dill

Zest of 1 lemon

1 tbsp freshly squeezed lemon juice, plus extra as needed

Cold-pressed olive oil, to serve

1 In a medium saucepan, heat the coconut oil over a medium heat. Add the onions and a pinch of salt. Cook until the onions have softened, about 5 minutes. Add the garlic and stir, cooking for a further 2 minutes.

2 Add the peas and vegetable stock. Cook for 1–2 minutes just until the peas are bright green and no longer frozen.

3 Quickly but carefully ladle the soup into a blender. Add the dill, lemon zest and juice. Blend on high until completely smooth. Taste and adjust the seasoning, if necessary.

4 Transfer the soup to a saucepan and heat until hot. Serve with a drizzle of olive oil.

ROLLOVER Use any leftover soup in the Cool It Noodle Salad with Radishes and Peas (page 104) instead of the Spicy Tahini Ginger Sauce – it will change up the flavour profile and create a totally different and delicious dish!

SPROUTED MUNG BEAN GAZPACHO

250 g / 9 oz cherry tomatoes

1 medium cucumber

1 red pepper, stem, seeds and ribs removed

60 g / 2¼ oz mung bean sprouts (recipe follows)

2 tbsp cold-pressed olive oil, plus extra for drizzling

½ tsp fine sea salt, plus extra as needed

750 g / 1 lb 10 oz Roma tomatoes

1 garlic clove

½ tsp freshly ground black pepper, plus extra as needed

1 tbsp freshly squeezed lemon juice

1 tbsp freshly squeezed lime juice

1–2 tsp apple cider vinegar, plus extra if liked

Grilled crusty wholegrain bread, to serve (optional)

Gazpacho is *the* classic summer soup, but I've changed things a little by adding mung bean sprouts to deliver a totally unique flavour and texture. As a bonus, you'll be getting far more protein, fibre and phytonutrients.

Because produce varies so widely according to seasonality and availability, this recipe should be used more as a guide than as a strict prescription. I find that playing with the salt and acidity levels is important to the success of this soup, so up the salt and vinegar until you achieve a tasty balance that suits your palate.

Any sprouts will work here if you don't have mung beans; just remember that sprouts take about three days to grow, so start this recipe ahead of time!

SERVES 4 ————————————————————————————

1 Finely dice half the cherry tomatoes, half the cucumber and half the red pepper.

2 In a medium bowl, combine the diced vegetables with the mung bean sprouts, a drizzle of olive oil and a pinch of salt. Stir and set aside.

3 Roughly chop the Roma tomatoes and place them in a blender with the remaining cherry tomatoes, cucumber and pepper, plus the garlic, ½ teaspoon of salt, black pepper, 2 tablespoons of oil, citrus juices and vinegar. Blend on high until smooth. Taste and adjust the flavours.

4 Transfer the gazpacho to a large serving bowl and add almost all of the diced vegetable–mung bean mixture, reserving a few spoonfuls for garnish. Place in the fridge to chill for at least 1 hour to allow the flavours to meld.

5 Ladle the soup into bowls and top with the remaining diced vegetable–mung bean mixture. Serve with the grilled wholegrain bread.

ROLLOVER Sprout extra mung beans to make the Sprouted Mung Bean and Mango Avocado Cups (page 67).

BASIC SPROUTS

MAKES ABOUT 100 G / 3½ OZ

I go into more detail about sprouting on my blog, but it's really a simple process.

(V) (GF) (R) (GrF)

2 tbsp seeds, beans or lentils

1 Place the seeds in a clean glass jar and fill it almost to the top with water. Cover the jar with a piece of muslin and secure it with a rubber band. Leave the seeds to soak at room temperature for 8–12 hours, or overnight.

2 Drain and rinse the seeds through the muslin 2 or 3 times. Set the jar upside down at a 45° angle in a bowl or dish rack to drain completely. Keep the seeds away from light or cover the glass with clean kitchen towel.

3 Repeat the rinsing and draining upside down at a 45° angle 2 or 3 times daily for 2–4 days until the seeds grow a good tail (at least 2 times longer than the seed itself).

4 Once the seeds have sprouted to your liking, rinse and drain the sprouts completely and let them sit out in a colander for at least 8 hours before adding them back to the jar, covering with an airtight lid, and storing them in the fridge for up to 2 weeks.

CHILL-OUT CUCUMBER AND AVOCADO SOUP

with Mint and Dukkah

2 cucumbers, roughly chopped

2 ripe avocados, flesh scooped out

3 tbsp freshly squeezed lemon juice

15 g / ½ oz fresh mint leaves

1 tsp fine sea salt

1 tbsp cold-pressed olive oil

15 g / ½ oz chopped fresh chives

7 g / ¼ oz chopped fresh flat-leaf parsley

250 ml / 8 fl oz water

Dukkah, to serve (optional; recipe follows)

When summertime hits, I miss soup like a long-lost friend. This year, I decided to chill out and find a new solution besides my beloved gazpacho (page 22), and I came up with this incredible concoction. Creamy avocado and crisp cucumber make the most amazing blend, especially when combined with lemon and mint. Dukkah – an Egyptian herb, nut and spice mixture – is the ideal accompaniment, grounding a dish that is otherwise raw and quite light. Sesame Salt (page 157) would also be delicious with this soup. If your blender is not very powerful, try straining the soup through a sieve to achieve extra smoothness.

SERVES 3–4

1 In a blender, combine the cucumbers, avocados, lemon juice, mint leaves, salt, oil, chives, parsley and water, and blend on high until the mixture is as smooth as possible. Strain through a fine sieve for extra smoothness, if liked. Season with salt.

2 Place in the fridge to chill for at least 2 hours to allow the flavours to meld. Enjoy cold, topped with Dukkah, if liked.

ROLLOVER Use the leftover Dukkah for the So-simple Roasted Roots with Dukkah (page 183).

(recipe continues)

140 g / 5 oz raw, unsalted hazelnuts

1 tbsp coriander seeds

1½ tsp cumin seeds

1 tbsp whole black peppercorns

75 g / 2¾ oz raw, unsalted sesame seeds

1 tsp fine sea salt, plus extra as needed

DUKKAH

MAKES ABOUT 225 G / 8 OZ

1 Preheat the oven to 160°C / 325°F / Gas mark 3. Spread the hazelnuts out in a single layer on a rimmed baking sheet and roast for 20–30 minutes until fragrant and the skins have turned darker in colour. (Another good way to check for doneness is to bite a hazelnut in half and inspect the colour – it should be golden, not white, inside.) Remove from the oven, and when cool enough to handle, rub the nuts together to remove the skins. Place the nuts in a food processor.

2 While the hazelnuts are roasting, preheat a dry frying pan over a medium heat. When hot, toast the coriander and cumin seeds, stirring frequently, until fragrant, about 2 minutes. Remove the pan from the heat immediately, leave the seeds to cool, then place them in a mortar and pestle and add the peppercorns. Using the pestle, grind the seeds and peppercorns together until pulverized. (Alternatively, grind them together in a coffee mill or food processor.) Set aside.

3 In the same frying pan, toast the sesame seeds for about 2 minutes until they are fragrant and begin to pop. Leave to cool slightly. Place the sesame seeds in the food processor with the hazelnuts. Pulse to chop the mixture until you get a chunky-sand texture. (Do not blend, or you will end up with hazelnut-sesame butter! Tasty, but not what we're after.)

4 Add the pulverized spices and the salt to the food processor and pulse once more to combine. Taste and adjust the seasonings, if necessary. Store in an airtight glass container at room temperature for up to 1 month.

LUXURIOUS CREAM OF MUSHROOM SOUP

with Garlic-herb Croûtons

The only cream of mushroom soup I ate as a kid was the canned variety – the one that plopped out of its claustrophobic aluminium home and retained its cylindrical-tin shape. You know the one I mean.

These days, I still love mushroom soup, but I make it from scratch without dairy. What is the secret to the creaminess without the cream? By blending cooked beans with vegetable stock, you end up with a totally luxurious texture that mimics double cream but is virtually fat-free. In addition, beans deliver healthy, vegetarian protein and a serious dose of filling fibre. It tastes as if you are eating the richest soup of all time, but it's a delicious illusion that warms you up, fills you up, but doesn't fill you out!

To take this delicious soup to the next level, you *must* make the Garlic-herb Croûtons. They are ridiculously rich, perfectly seasoned and extra crunchy. You'll be finding reasons to make soup just to eat them!

SERVES 4 ————————————————————

1 To prepare the leek, cut the white and light-green parts in half lengthways and then crossways into chunks.

2 In a large stockpot or saucepan, melt the coconut oil over a medium heat. Add the onions, leek, salt, black pepper, thyme and bay leaves. Cook for 5 minutes until the onions and leeks are soft. Very finely chop the garlic, add it to the pot and stir.

3 While the onions, leeks and garlic are cooking, clean the mushrooms by removing any dirt or natural debris with a damp cloth (do not wash them in water). Cut the mushrooms into quarters and add them to the pot. Cook for 10–15 minutes until they are dark brown and very soft. Add the stock and stir.

1 large leek

1 tbsp coconut oil or ghee

3 medium yellow onions, chopped

1 tsp fine sea salt, plus extra as needed

1 tsp freshly ground black pepper, plus extra as needed

2 tsp fresh thyme leaves (or 1 tsp dried), plus extra to garnish

4 bay leaves

4 garlic cloves

400 g / 14 oz chestnut mushrooms

500 ml / 18 fl oz vegetable stock

250 ml / 8 fl oz plant-based milk of your choice

250 g / 9 oz (about 1 400 g / 14 oz can) white beans, such as haricot, butter or cannellini, drained and rinsed

1½ tsp balsamic vinegar

Garlic-herb Croûtons (recipe follows)

(recipe continues)

4 Meanwhile, combine the milk and beans in a blender and blend on high until smooth.

5 When the mushrooms are cooked, add the vinegar and about one-third of the soup to the blender with the blended beans. Blend on high until creamy, then pour the mixture back into the pot with the remaining soup, stir well and reduce the heat to low. Simmer for 5 minutes. Thin the soup with water, if liked.

6 Season with plenty of freshly ground black pepper and sea salt. Ladle the soup into bowls and sprinkle with the croûtons and some fresh thyme sprigs.

ROLLOVER Make extra croûtons and use them for the Grilled Caesar Salad instead of the Chickpea Croûtons (page 61).

GARLIC-HERB CROÛTONS

MAKES 330 G / 11½ OZ

1 Preheat the oven to 160°C / 325°F / Gas mark 3.

2 In a small saucepan, melt the coconut oil over a medium heat. Add the garlic and onion powders, thyme, oregano and salt, whisking to combine.

3 Place the bread cubes on a rimmed baking sheet and pour the oil mixture over the top, tossing very well to coat the bread. Bake for 25–45 minutes until the croûtons are golden, fully toasted and dry. Store leftovers in an airtight glass jar at room temperature for up to 2 weeks.

1½ tsp coconut oil

½ tsp garlic powder

½ tsp onion powder

¼ tsp dried thyme

¼ tsp dried oregano

¼ tsp fine sea salt

330 g / 11½ oz cubed wholegrain bread (sourdough, if possible)

NORTH AFRICAN SUN-DRIED TOMATO SOUP

with Couscous Topping

SOUP

1 tbsp coconut oil or ghee

3 yellow onions, chopped

2 pinches of fine sea salt

3 garlic cloves, finely chopped

2 tsp ground cumin

1 tsp ground cinnamon

2 tsp ground coriander

1 tbsp peeled, finely chopped fresh ginger

1 tbsp gluten-free harissa paste (available at Middle Eastern grocery stores)

2 large red peppers (stems, seeds and ribs removed), chopped

1.2–1.5 litres / 2–2½ pints vegetable stock

1 400 g / 14 oz can whole tomatoes

100 g / 3½ oz chopped sun-dried tomatoes

225 g / 8 oz (1 240 g / 8½ oz can) cooked chickpeas, drained and rinsed

COUSCOUS TOPPING

90 g / 3¼ oz wholewheat

This hearty dish is a perfect meal to enjoy when the first autumn days are creeping in and you need a little cosiness, but you can also enjoy it cold. By using a combination of sun-dried and canned tomatoes, you'll add tons of umami notes to a totally vegan soup. The texture of the couscous topping provides a welcoming contrast to the smooth purée, while the olives lend a salty bite and the parsley adds a fresh note. Harissa is a Tunisian hot chilli paste. It's easy to make (the recipe is on the *My New Roots* blog!), or look for it pre-made at the supermarket. If you do not have harissa paste, simply add some cayenne pepper or smoked hot paprika, as desired.

SERVES 4–6

1 Start the soup: in a large stockpot, melt the coconut oil over a medium heat. Add the onions and salt and stir to coat. Cook, stirring occasionally, until the onions soften and begin to slightly caramelize, about 10 minutes. Add the garlic, cumin, cinnamon, coriander, ginger and harissa paste and cook for about 2 minutes until fragrant. Add the peppers and cook for 5 minutes, adding a little stock to the pot if the mixture becomes dry.

2 Add the whole tomatoes and their juices along with the sun-dried tomatoes and the rest of the stock. Bring to the boil, reduce the heat to low and cook for 15 minutes.

3 Carefully transfer the soup to a blender and blend on high until smooth. Return the soup to the pot, add the chickpeas and heat through.

4 Meanwhile, make the couscous topping: in a small pot, combine the couscous and the salt, and cook according to the packet instructions. Fluff with a fork, then add the olives, parsley, lemon zest and juice and olive oil. Season with salt.

5 To serve, ladle the soup into bowls and top with as much couscous as desired. Enjoy hot or cold.

ROLLOVER Use extra sun-dried tomatoes in the Smoked Lentil Tacos with Pico de Gallo (page 112).

COUSCOUS

¼ tsp fine sea salt

75 g / 2¾ oz chopped black olives

15 g / ½ oz chopped fresh flat-leaf parsley

Zest of 1 lemon

1½ tsp freshly squeezed lemon juice

1 tbsp olive oil

GINGER-LEMON
SPLIT PEA SOUP

My father-in-law is obsessed with traditions. Birthdays, holidays, weddings, graduations. . . he's there to make the day special and momentous, and, of course, to remind us all of the elaborate ways we need to carry out the proceedings *just* how everything was done the last time – because it's tradition. The last weekend in November, when all of Denmark is mourning the very last bits of light before winter, it is a tradition that we gather at my father-in-law's house for yellow split pea soup. For me, sitting round a long table with my large extended family, catching up over piping-hot bowls of golden soup is an antidote to the darkness and softens the blow of impending cold.

This is my version of the soup, which I continue to make from that weekend deep into the winter months to remedy whatever chill has taken hold. Split peas are relatively bland, so this soup relies on plenty of ginger and lemon for brightness, and pumpkin to bring sweetness and depth – certainly non-traditional but delicious additions. I like to crush a few pieces of the cooked pumpkin on the side of the pot with my wooden spoon and let it dissolve into the stock; it acts as a thickener and turns the soup a lovely golden hue.

SERVES 4

1 Melt the coconut oil in a large stockpot or pan over a medium heat. Add the onions, leeks and salt and stir to coat. Cook for 10 minutes, stirring occasionally, until the onions soften and begin to caramelize. Add the garlic, ginger, turmeric, bay, celery, pumpkin and peas. Toss to coat, then add the stock. Bring to the boil, reduce the heat to low and simmer, covered, for 30–40 minutes until the peas and pumpkin are tender.

2 Just before serving, add the lemon juice and season with salt. Ladle the soup into bowls and top with a slice of lemon, if using.

V · GF · GrF

1 tbsp coconut oil or ghee

3 medium yellow onions, diced

1 leek, white and light-green parts, chopped

1 tsp fine sea salt

5 garlic cloves, finely chopped

3 tbsp peeled, finely chopped fresh ginger

1½ tsp ground turmeric

3 bay leaves

3 celery sticks, diced

500 g / 1 lb 2 oz pumpkin, chopped into cubes (sweet potatoes will also work)

200 g / 7 oz yellow split peas, soaked if possible, drained and rinsed

1.5 litres / 2½ pints vegetable stock

Freshly squeezed juice of 1 lemon, plus a few slices to garnish (optional)

ROLLOVER If you have any leftover ginger, make the Ginger-pickled Carrots (page 87).

GARLIC CLOUD SOUP

40 garlic cloves
(3–4 whole heads)

3 medium yellow onions

1 head of cauliflower

2 tbsp coconut oil or ghee,
melted

1 tsp fine sea salt, plus extra
as needed

500 ml / 18 fl oz vegetable
stock

500 ml / 18 fl oz plant-
based milk of your choice

1½ tsp freshly squeezed
lemon juice

Cold-pressed olive oil, to
serve

Let me start off by saying that, yes, this recipe calls for forty cloves of garlic and, no, I haven't totally lost my mind. This ethereally creamy, dreamy soup is for immune boosting and deep healing. Keep this recipe in your flu-busting arsenal, or whip some up right when you feel the sniffles coming on. Roasting the garlic this way really mellows out its sharpness, and I promise you can still be social after eating it!

SERVES 4

1 Preheat the oven to 200°C / 400°F / Gas mark 6.

2 Peel the garlic cloves and quarter the onions, and place them on a baking sheet. Cut up the cauliflower into bite-sized chunks and add it to the garlic and onions. Drizzle with the melted coconut oil and toss to coat. Sprinkle with ½ teaspoon of sea salt. Roast for 25–30 minutes until everything has golden edges and is nicely caramelized.

3 Leave the veggies to cool slightly and then add to a blender along with the vegetable stock, milk, remaining ½ teaspoon of salt and lemon juice (process in batches if you have a small blender). Blend on high until as smooth as possible. Taste and adjust the seasonings, if necessary.

4 If the soup is not hot enough after blending, transfer it to a large pan and warm until steaming. If the soup is too thick, simply add water to thin to your desired consistency. Serve hot with a drizzle of olive oil.

COCONUT ZINGER
BLACK BEAN SOUP

1 tbsp coconut oil

2 tsp ground cumin

1 tsp ground coriander

¼ tsp cayenne pepper

2 yellow onions, diced

½ tsp fine sea salt

5 garlic cloves, finely
chopped

1 heaped tbsp peeled, finely
chopped fresh ginger

500 g / 1 lb 2 oz sweet
potatoes (about 2 large),
scrubbed and chopped

750 ml / 1¼ pints vegetable
stock or water

1 400 ml / 14 fl oz can full-
fat coconut milk

500 g / 1 lb 2 oz (2 400 g
/ 14 oz cans) cooked black
beans, drained and rinsed

2–3 tbsp freshly squeezed
lime juice

2 handfuls of fresh coriander
leaves and tender stems,
chopped

Cold-pressed olive oil, to
serve

ROLLOVER Cook extra
black beans for the Quinoa
and Black Beans with Radish
Coriander Salsa (page 106).

When you need something in your belly quick, this soup will not disappoint. With a couple of sweet potatoes, a can of coconut milk and some cooked black beans that I had stashed in the freezer, I whipped this up so fast that I even shocked myself! The black beans and coconut are a surprising yet delightful combination, and, of course, with fibre-rich and tasty sweet potatoes we're all winners.

This soup needs a surprising amount of acid, in this case lime juice, to balance the sweetness of the coconut milk and sweet potatoes. Add it to your liking, and taste the results as you go. You can also make this as spicy as you like. The amount of cayenne I've indicated gives a medium heat level, but feel free to blow your head off.

SERVES 4–6 ————————————————————————

1 In a large stockpot, melt the coconut oil over a medium heat. Add the cumin, coriander and cayenne and cook for about 2 minutes, stirring constantly, until fragrant. Add the onions and salt, and stir to coat. Cook, stirring occasionally, for 5–7 minutes until the onions have softened.

2 Add the garlic and ginger and cook for 2 minutes; if the pot becomes dry at any point, add a little water or stock. Add the sweet potatoes, stock and coconut milk.

3 Cover the pot and bring the soup to the boil, then reduce the heat to low and simmer for 10–15 minutes until the potatoes are tender. Add half of the black beans and simmer until they have warmed through.

4 Transfer about half of the soup to a blender and purée until completely smooth. Add the lime juice. Pour the blended soup back into the pot and add the remaining whole black beans. Season with salt. Serve hot, garnished with plenty of chopped coriander and a drizzle of olive oil.

CASHEW CORN CHOWDER
with Chipotle Oil

1 tbsp coconut oil or ghee

1 tbsp ground turmeric

2 tsp ground cumin

2 pinches of cayenne pepper

3 medium yellow onions, chopped

2 tsp fine sea salt, plus extra as needed

6 garlic cloves, very finely chopped

1 litre / 1¾ pints vegetable stock

4 fresh corn cobs

93 g / 3¼ oz raw cashews, soaked for at least 4 hours or up to overnight

1 tbsp freshly squeezed lime juice

2 tbsp cold-pressed olive oil

¼ tsp ground chipotle

Handful of fresh coriander leaves and tender stems, to garnish

Classic chowder relies heavily on milk and cream, and perhaps a little butter for extra unctuousness. As yum as that is, if you have never used cashews to replace regular cream or milk in a soup before, I highly recommend you try it with this comfort food classic. I've also added a drizzle of chipotle oil for kick and a handful of herbaceous coriander to take this soup to the next level. Spicy-sweet Pumpkin Seed Snacks (page 211) sprinkled over the top would be delicious too.

SERVES 4 ——————————————————————————

1 Melt the coconut oil in a large pan over a medium heat. Add the turmeric, cumin and cayenne, and cook for about 1 minute until fragrant. Add the onions and salt and cook for about 5 minutes until softened. Add the garlic. If the base of the pan becomes dry, add a little stock to moisten things up.

2 Meanwhile, cut off the kernels of the corn by standing each cob on its end in a shallow bowl and slicing downwards. Add the corn kernels to the pan and stir to coat with the spices. Cook for 5 minutes, then add the remaining stock. Bring to the boil, then reduce the heat to low and simmer for 5 minutes until the corn is bright yellow and sweet.

3 Once the corn is cooked, remove the pan from the heat and transfer the soup to a blender, reserving a few tablespoons of the whole corn kernels for garnish. Add the soaked and rinsed cashews and the lime juice. Blend on high until smooth. Add water to thin the soup if liked. Season with salt. If not serving straight away, return the soup to the pan to keep warm.

4 In a small bowl, whisk the olive oil with the chipotle until thoroughly blended. Serve the soup with a drizzle of chipotle oil, a sprinkle of coriander and the reserved corn kernels.

ROLLOVER Use leftover coriander for the Radish Coriander Salsa (page 108).

BROCCOLI BASIL BROTH

with Noodles and Sesame Salt

1 tbsp plus 1 tsp fine sea salt

170 g / 6 oz dried gluten-free or wholegrain noodles of your choice

5 garlic cloves

1 tbsp coconut oil or ghee

3 medium yellow onions, chopped

1 litre / 1¾ pints vegetable stock

1 large head of broccoli, stalk removed and florets separated

2–3 tbsp freshly squeezed lime juice

1 tbsp pure maple syrup

1 tbsp peeled, finely chopped fresh ginger

25 g / 1 oz basil leaves; reserve a couple leaves to garnish

Cold-pressed olive oil, to serve

Sesame Salt (optional; page 157)

If you're a parent, you'll understand the feeling of relief, accomplishment and utter joy when your child eats something healthy. Although broccoli and basil don't seem like the most likely of pals, when my discriminating one-and-a-half-year-old son hoovers the combo, I am not going to argue. The secret to making broccoli taste great is not to overcook it, which brings out its sulfuric compounds. My method only allows the broccoli to bathe in hot stock for five minutes before a big blend-up, instead of boiling it to death.

SERVES 4 ——————————————————————————

1 Fill a medium saucepan with water and bring to the boil. Add 1 tablespoon of the sea salt and the pasta, and cook until al dente, according to the packet instructions. Drain and cover to keep warm.

2 Finely chop the garlic (no need to be too precise, since you'll be blending everything). In a large stockpot or pan, melt the coconut oil over a medium heat. Add the onions and remaining teaspoon of salt and stir to coat. Cook for about 10 minutes, stirring occasionally, until the onions soften and begin to slightly caramelize. Add the garlic and cook for about 2 minutes until fragrant.

3 Add the stock, bring to the boil and reduce the heat to low. Add the broccoli, remove the pot from the heat and leave to stand for 5 minutes.

4 Transfer the soup to a blender and blend on high until smooth. Add the lime juice, maple syrup, ginger and basil leaves. Blend on high until incorporated. Season with salt.

5 Portion out the noodles into four bowls. Ladle the soup over the top, garnish with basil and drizzle with olive oil. Sprinkle with Sesame Salt, if liked.

ROLLOVER: Cook extra noodles to make the Cool It Noodle Salad with Radishes and Peas (page 104).

DEEP DETOX CORIANDER, SPINACH AND SWEET POTATO SOUP

I originally created this recipe for a January detoxification post on my blog, but I love it so much that I make it all the time – even when I'm not on a cleanse! It is rich and hearty with tons of brightness from the lemon and coriander, plus a little kick from the cayenne pepper. Even though it's super green, there is no flavour sacrifice here. Just another rad example of how food that tastes amazing can just 'happen' to be healthy.

SERVES 4

1 In a large stockpot or pan, melt the coconut oil over a medium heat. Add the onions and salt, stir to coat and cook for 5–7 minutes until the onions have softened. Add the garlic, stir and cook for a further 1 minute. Add the sweet potatoes and water. Bring the soup to the boil, then reduce the heat to low and simmer for 12–15 minutes until the sweet potatoes are tender.

2 Transfer the soup to a blender. Blend on high until smooth, then add the spinach, coriander, lemon and cayenne and continue blending until smooth. Season with salt. Store cooled leftovers in the fridge for up to 3 days.

1 tbsp coconut oil

2 medium yellow onions, chopped

1 tsp fine sea salt

4–5 garlic cloves, finely chopped (to suit your taste)

2 medium-large sweet potatoes, scrubbed and cut into 2.5 cm / 1 in cubes

750 ml / 1¼ pints water

50 g / 1¾ oz fresh baby spinach

60 g / 2¼ oz fresh coriander leaves and tender stems

1 tbsp freshly squeezed lemon juice

1 pinch–¼ tsp cayenne pepper

RED VELVET ROASTED GARLIC BEETROOT SOUP

with Mustard-spiked Yogurt

1 kg / 2 lb 4 oz beetroot

1 head of garlic

1 tbsp plus ½ tsp coconut oil

3 leeks

1 tsp fine sea salt

2 tsp dried thyme

3 bay leaves

1 litre / 1¾ pints vegetable stock

1 tbsp freshly squeezed lemon juice

½ tsp freshly ground black pepper

125 g / 4½ oz plain yogurt (preferably goat's or sheep's)

1 tsp Dijon mustard

ROLLOVER Roast extra beetroot for the Rainbow Hummus Bowl (page 74).

Roasting beetroot is a simple process that transforms the earthy, crunchy roots into silky, sweet, tender globes. Although you can steam and boil them, roasting concentrates their flavours and makes them much sweeter. I've taken advantage of the long cooking time to roast garlic too, which pairs so well with beetroot. Blended all together, this soup is so velvety.

SERVES 4–6

1 Preheat the oven to 200°C / 400°F / Gas mark 6. Wrap each beetroot in foil and place on a baking sheet. Slice off the portion just below the garlic bulb stem, revealing the cloves. Spread ½ teaspoon of the coconut oil on top, wrap the bulb in foil and set on the baking sheet. Roast for about 45 minutes until the beetroot is tender when pierced with a knife.

2 Meanwhile, remove the dark-green tops of the leeks, slice the white and light-green parts in half lengthways and rinse well to remove any dirt. Slice the leeks crossways into chunks.

3 In a large stockpot, melt the remaining 1 tablespoon of coconut oil over a medium heat. Add the leeks and a few pinches of sea salt and stir. Add the thyme and bay leaves. Cook for 5 minutes until the leeks soften.

4 When the beetroot is cool enough to handle, slip off the skins, cut them into chunks and add to the pot with the leeks. Add the stock, bring to the boil, reduce the heat and simmer for 3–4 minutes until the leeks are soft.

5 Remove the foil from the garlic and squeeze the bulb to extract the cloves into a blender. Discard the bay leaves from the pot. Add the beetroot mixture and lemon juice to the blender and mix on high until smooth. Season with the pepper. In a separate dish, stir the yogurt and mustard together, swirl into each bowl of soup and enjoy.

GOLDEN CURRY COCONUT DAL

This soup was born at a restaurant where I worked called Morgenstedet (The Morning Place), which didn't make much sense because we opened at noon for lunch. We served vegetarian soups, salads, rice dishes and casseroles – heartwarming home-style food that drew large crowds every day of the year. I found the sheer quantity of food I had to make there incredibly daunting (I could quite literally sit in the soup pots!), and I was always pressed for time in the kitchen. This soup became my saviour because it was so fast and easy to whip up, but it never tasted that way. In fact, on more occasions than I can count, people told me just how deep and delicious it was – I kept my secrets of simplicity to myself.

Double or triple the recipe – it tastes amazing the day after and freezes exceptionally well, or add more vegetables if you like: green peas, sweet potatoes and pumpkin are especially tasty.

SERVES 4

1 In a large stockpot or pan, melt the coconut oil over a medium-high heat. Add the onions and salt, stir to coat and cook for about 10 minutes until the onions soften and begin to slightly caramelize.

2 Add the garlic, ginger, cumin, curry powder and turmeric. Stir well and cook for about 3 minutes until fragrant, adding a little stock to the pot if it becomes too dry.

3 Add the lentils, carrots, tomatoes, coconut milk and remaining stock. Bring to the boil, reduce the heat to low and simmer for about 20 minutes until the lentils are tender. If the tomatoes remain whole after cooking, give them a squish against the side of the pot with a spoon to break them up a little.

4 Just before serving, stir in the lime juice, a little at a time, until the flavours are to your liking. Season with salt and serve with the coriander.

1 tbsp coconut oil or ghee

3 medium yellow onions, diced

2 tsp fine sea salt, plus extra as needed

5 garlic cloves, finely chopped

1 tbsp peeled, finely chopped fresh ginger

1 tsp ground cumin

1 tbsp curry powder

1 tsp ground turmeric

750 ml / 1¼ pints vegetable stock

200 g / 7 oz red lentils, washed and drained

3 medium carrots, chopped

1 400 g / 14 oz can whole tomatoes

1 400 ml / 14 fl oz can full-fat coconut milk

1–2 tbsp freshly squeezed lime juice, plus extra as needed

Handful of fresh coriander leaves and tender stems, to serve

CLEVER PARSNIP OVEN SOUP

1 small head of garlic

½ tsp coconut oil or ghee

1 kg / 2 lb 4 oz parsnips

3 medium yellow onions

1.5 litres / 2½ pints
vegetable stock or water

250 g / 9 oz (about 1
400 g / 14 oz can) white
beans, such as cannellini or
haricot, drained and rinsed

1–2 tsp fine sea salt (use 1
tsp if using stock; 2 tsp if
using water)

1 tbsp cold-pressed olive oil,
plus extra to serve

1 tbsp freshly squeezed
lemon juice

Freshly ground black pepper,
to serve

The process for this soup is incredibly easy: all the ingredients are placed on a rimmed baking sheet, and the oven does the work. There isn't even a pot to wash when the meal's over. You can use this procedure with any veggies, plus onions and garlic. Just add everything to a blender directly from the oven, pour in some hot vegetable stock and dinner is served. Bam!

SERVES 6 ────────────────────────────

1 Preheat the oven to 200°C / 400°F / Gas mark 6. Slice off the stem of the garlic bulb and the portion just below the stem, revealing the open cloves. Spread the coconut oil on top, wrap the bulb tightly in foil and set it on a rimmed baking sheet. Roast for 15 minutes.

2 While the garlic is roasting, peel and roughly cut the parsnips into similarly sized chunks to ensure even roasting. Chop the onions. After the garlic has roasted for 15 minutes, add the parsnips and onions to the baking sheet. Roast for about 30 minutes until tender.

3 Place the roasted parsnips and onions in a blender. Remove the foil from the garlic and squeeze the bulb from the bottom to extract the cloves into the blender. Add the stock, beans, salt, olive oil and lemon juice and blend on the highest setting until the soup is smooth and creamy. Transfer the soup to a stockpot or saucepan and heat until steaming, if necessary.

4 Serve hot with a drizzle of olive oil and some black pepper.

sumptuous
SALADS

PREVIOUS PAGE, from left to right: Roasted Sweet Potato and Butter Beans on Massaged Kale, page 54 / Massaged Kale Pressed Salad, page 56 / Harissa-dressed Massaged Kale, page 55

MASSAGED KALE, 3 WAYS

In recent years we've seen a maniacal surge in the popularity of fermented foods, coconut water and 'putting an egg on it', but the biggest trend of all is kale. It seems as if every restaurant menu and every cookbook and food blog (including mine) has incorporated the king of green – and who's complaining? Certainly not me! Trends can be silly, sure, but this is one craze I can get behind. My favourite way to enjoy kale is by massaging it, which turns kale into a delicate, tender, dark-green delight that will keep well in the fridge for up to a week.

Here, too, is a recipe for a pressed salad, which is a classic macrobiotic technique that uses salt to help break down some of the hard-to-digest fibres of the vegetables. After massaging the vegetables, which releases their water, you press them down with a plate to mix the water with the salt, which essentially dresses the salad, so you don't need any other sauce besides a light squeeze of lemon, if you wish. Pressed salads are easy to make, versatile and incredibly delicious! Change the ingredients to suit the season. These recipes are my love letter to massaged kale – three ways to take this tender, verdant base in different directions.

ROLLOVER Massage extra kale to use in Ceremonial Stuffed Pumpkin with Bulgur Wheat, Feta and Figs (page 143).

SALAD

1 large sweet potato

1 tsp coconut oil, melted

¾ tsp fine sea salt, plus extra as needed

120 g / 4¼ oz shredded curly kale (shredding how-to included)

1 tbsp cold-pressed olive oil, plus extra as needed

1 tbsp freshly squeezed lemon juice

1 small red onion, thinly sliced

45 g / 1½ oz raw, unsalted pumpkin seeds

225 g / 8 oz (1 240 g / 8½ oz can) cooked butter beans, drained and rinsed

LEMON GARLIC DRESSING

1 small garlic clove, very finely chopped

2 tbsp cold-pressed olive oil

Zest of 1 lemon

2 tbsp freshly squeezed lemon juice

Pinch of fine sea salt

¼–½ tsp pure maple syrup or raw honey

ROASTED SWEET POTATO AND BUTTER BEANS
on Massaged Kale

SERVES 4 AS A MAIN, 6 AS A SIDE ————————————————

1 Prepare the salad: preheat the oven to 200°C / 400°F / Gas mark 6. Peel the sweet potato (if it's not organic) and cut it into cubes. Place the cubes on a rimmed baking sheet and toss with the melted coconut oil and ¼ teaspoon of sea salt. Roast for 15–20 minutes until tender. Leave to cool and then put the cubes into a large bowl or serving platter.

2 Meanwhile, wash the kale well and spin it dry. Remove the stems and tough ribs, roll the leaves into a cigar shape and slice crossways to make ribbons. In a large bowl, combine the kale ribbons with the olive oil, ½ teaspoon of salt and the lemon juice. Using your hands, rub and squeeze the kale together as if you are giving it a massage for about 2 minutes until the kale leaves are dark green and tender. Add the kale to the sweet potato cubes. Sprinkle the onion slices over the top.

3 Preheat a small dry frying pan over a medium heat. When hot, toast the pumpkin seeds for 3–5 minutes, tossing frequently, until fragrant. Remove the pan from the heat immediately, leave the seeds to cool, then crush them with a mortar and pestle, if liked (crushed seeds add a nice texture to the salad).

4 Make the dressing: in a small bowl, whisk together the garlic, olive oil, lemon zest and juice, salt and maple syrup.

5 Finish the salad: place the beans in a medium bowl. Pour half of the dressing over the beans, stir well to coat and let them marinate for 5–10 minutes. Add the marinated beans to the kale, sweet potato and red onion. Pour the remaining dressing over the top, sprinkle with the pumpkin seeds and serve.

HARISSA-DRESSED MASSAGED KALE

SERVES 4 AS A MAIN, 6 AS A SIDE ──────────

1 Prepare the salad: wash the kale well and spin it dry. Remove the stems and tough ribs, roll the leaves into a cigar shape and slice crossways to make ribbons. In a large bowl, combine the kale ribbons with the olive oil, salt and lemon juice. Using your hands, rub and squeeze the kale together as if you are giving it a massage for about 2 minutes until the kale leaves are dark green and tender.

2 Make the dressing: in a small bowl, whisk together the harissa, olive oil, lemon juice, maple syrup and salt.

3 Finish the salad: using a vegetable peeler or mandoline, slice the carrots lengthways into long, thin ribbons. Add the carrots, feta and raisins to the kale. Pour the dressing over the top, lightly toss the ingredients together and serve.

SALAD

240 g / 8½ oz curly kale, shredded (shredding how-to included)

2 tbsp cold-pressed olive oil

½ tsp fine sea salt

2 tbsp freshly squeezed lemon juice

2 large carrots

100 g / 3½ oz feta (preferably goat's or sheep's), crumbled

35 g / 1¼ oz raisins, roughly chopped

HARISSA DRESSING

4 tsp gluten-free harissa paste (available at Middle Eastern grocery stores)

3 tbsp cold-pressed olive oil

2 tsp freshly squeezed lemon juice

¼ tsp pure maple syrup or raw honey

Pinch of fine sea salt

240g / 8½ oz curly kale, shredded (shredding how-to included)

1 kg / 2 lb 4 oz mixed vegetables (I recommend ½ small head of red cabbage, 1 large carrot, 1 small sweet potato, 1 small fennel bulb and 1 small red onion)

1 small apple

1½ tsp peeled, very finely chopped fresh ginger

2 tsp fine sea salt

Juice of 1 lemon

TO SERVE

Handful of fresh flat-leaf parsley

Handful of fresh coriander leaves and tender stems

Sesame Salt (optional; page 157)

Lemon wedges

Cold-pressed olive oil

MASSAGED KALE PRESSED SALAD

SERVES 4 AS A MAIN, 6 AS A SIDE —————————————

1 Prepare the salad: wash the kale and cabbage leaves well and spin them dry. Remove stems and tough ribs, roll the leaves into a cigar shape and slice them crossways to make ribbons. Combine them in a large bowl.

2 Using a julienne slicer (or good knife skills!), julienne the carrot, sweet potato, fennel, red onion and apple. Add the vegetables and ginger to the cabbage and kale. Sprinkle the salt over the top.

3 Using your hands, rub and squeeze everything together as if you are giving it a massage, until the vegetables begin to break down and release a great deal of their liquid when you squeeze a large handful. If there is not a lot of liquid, keep massaging.

4 Press the salad: place a plate directly on top of the massaged vegetables and weight it down with a heavy object, such as a litre jar filled with water. Leave the salad to press for about 30 minutes.

5 Finish the salad: just before serving, fold the lemon juice into the vegetables. Chop the parsley and coriander. Divide the salad among individual plates and sprinkle each portion with fresh herbs and Sesame Salt, if using. Serve with lemon wedges and olive oil. Once made, this salad keeps very well in the fridge for a few days.

SNAPPY SPRING SALAD

with Lemon-mint Date Sauce

I was recently catching up with an old friend who told me that her absolute favourite recipe on my blog was the Snappy Spring Salad, which is from a post so old that I had long forgotten about it. But her enthusiasm had me intrigued: what was it about this simple-sounding salad that was so darn delish? So I tried it again. And then I remembered. This is exactly what I feel like when the winter frost retreats and weather turns warm enough for things to grow again. It tastes fresh and alive, especially with the Lemon-mint Date Sauce, which is unreasonably delicious.

SERVES 4 AS A MAIN, 6 AS A SIDE ——————————

1 Make the quinoa: rinse the quinoa well. In a small saucepan, combine the quinoa, water and salt. Bring to the boil, reduce the heat to low and cook, covered, for about 20 minutes until all the water has been absorbed and the grains are tender. Fluff with a fork.

2 Prepare the vegetables: meanwhile, bring a pot of water to the boil. Add the peas and cook for 1–2 minutes until they are bright green. Quickly drain and run under cold water to halt the cooking. Wash the asparagus and snap off the thick ends where they naturally break. Using a vegetable peeler, slice the asparagus lengthways into long, thin ribbons.

3 Toast the seeds: preheat a dry frying pan over a medium heat. When hot, toast the pumpkin seeds for 3–5 minutes, tossing frequently, until fragrant. Remove the pan from the heat immediately and set aside.

4 Finish the salad: slice the radishes on the bias. In a large bowl, combine the cooked quinoa with the radishes, peas, asparagus and pumpkin seeds. Pour in about half of the sauce, season with a couple of pinches of fine sea salt and toss well. Taste and add more sauce if liked. Finish with a pinch or two of sea salt flakes.

QUINOA

170 g / 6 oz quinoa, soaked if possible

430 ml / 15 fl oz water

¾ tsp fine sea salt, plus extra as needed

VEGETABLES

150 g / 5½ oz green peas, fresh or frozen

450 g / 1 lb (1 bunch) asparagus

TO SERVE

60 g / 2¼ oz raw, unsalted pumpkin seeds

1 bunch (about 12) radishes

Lemon-mint Date Sauce (recipe follows)

Sea salt flakes

(recipe continues)

LEMON-MINT DATE SAUCE

MAKES ABOUT 250 ML / 8 FL OZ

1 Using a food processor or immersion blender, purée the lemon zest and juice, mint and dates until uniform in texture.

2 With the motor running, add the oil and then thin the sauce with a little water until you get a consistency that you can drizzle. Season with the salt. Store leftovers in an airtight jar in the fridge for up to 4 days.

ROLLOVER Cook 55 g / 2 oz extra quinoa for the Quinoa Corn Muffins (page 203).

Zest and juice of 2 lemons

20 g / ¾ oz fresh mint leaves

3–4 soft pitted dates

4 tbsp cold-pressed olive oil

Pinch of fine sea salt

GRILLED CAESAR SALAD

with Chickpea Croûtons

As your friend, I am telling you that grilling lettuce may change your life forever. And at the very least it'll revolutionize your salad. Romaine is a hearty beast that stands up to the grill's high heat, while its structure can hold its shape during cooking. This technique brings crazy flavour to a rather bland leaf, and the Chickpea Croûtons and Tahini Caesar Dressing take this dish to a place you've only dreamed of.

2 heads of romaine lettuce

Coconut oil, for rubbing

Fine sea salt

Tahini Caesar Dressing
(recipe follows)

Chickpea Croûtons
(recipe follows)

SERVES 2 AS A MAIN, 4 AS A SIDE —————————————

1 Remove the looser outer leaves from the romaine heads (and save them for another salad) so all that remains are the tighter, inner leaves. Cut off the top quarter of each head (and save the tops for another salad). Slice the head in half lengthways. Rub both the outsides and cut sides with a little coconut oil and sprinkle with a couple of pinches of sea salt.

2 Preheat a grill on high (a stovetop grill pan also works). When it is very hot, place the lettuce halves on the grill, cut-sides down, and cook for 3–4 minutes until charred and grill marks appear. Flip and cook for a further 2–3 minutes.

3 To serve, place a lettuce half on each plate and let guests dress and garnish the salads themselves. (The croûtons will soften quite quickly once in contact with the dressing, so it's best if diners add their own dressing.)

ROLLOVER Use the outer leaves and tops of the romaine lettuce in the Ginger-pickled Carrot Lentil Salad with Spiced Prunes and Dukkah (page 85).

(recipe continues)

125 ml / 4 fl oz tahini

1 garlic clove

½ tsp freshly ground black pepper

1 tbsp cold-pressed olive oil

Zest of 1 lemon

1 tbsp freshly squeezed lemon juice

2 tsp Dijon mustard

2 tsp gluten-free tamari

125 ml / 4 fl oz water

Fine sea salt

TAHINI CAESAR DRESSING

MAKES 125 ML / 4 FL OZ

In a blender, combine all the ingredients and blend on high until smooth, adding more water as necessary, up to 250 ml / 8 fl oz in total. Season with salt. Store leftover dressing in an airtight jar in the fridge for up to 1 week.

450 g / 1 lb (2 400 g / 14 oz cans) cooked chickpeas, drained and rinsed

3 tbsp coconut oil

1 tsp fine sea salt

1 tsp freshly ground black pepper

1 tsp garlic powder

CHICKPEA CROÛTONS

MAKES 750 G / 1 LB 10 OZ

1 Preheat the oven to 200°C / 400°F / Gas mark 6.

2 Spread the chickpeas out on a clean kitchen towel and rub them dry, discarding any loose skins. Pour the chickpeas into a medium bowl and toss with the coconut oil, salt, pepper and garlic powder.

3 Transfer the chickpeas to a rimmed baking sheet lined with baking paper, and roast for 25–35 minutes, stirring occasionally, until golden and crisp.

4 Remove the baking sheet from the oven. Leave the chickpeas to cool, and serve them at room temperature. They will crisp up quite a bit once they've cooled, so don't worry if they are still a little soft when you take them out of the oven. Store the chickpeas in an airtight glass container at room temperature for up to 1 week.

COCONUT-QUINOA COLESLAW

with Minty Tahini Dressing

My friend Henriette is one of the most talented (and humble!) cooks that I know. We worked together at an organic vegetarian restaurant for years, and I learned so much from her, including how to think outside of the box and try new combinations of foods, even if they seemed unusual. One day she was making a cabbage salad and folded in toasted coconut. I looked over at what she was doing and raised an eyebrow. . . you can't mess with coleslaw! But it worked. Ever since then, I love tossing a little coconut into my cabbage salads. It adds sweet, nutty notes, and its richness is the perfect balance for the lightness of the cabbage. My version includes quinoa for a meal-like salad, but this is optional. The smooth and creamy Minty Tahini Dressing is ridiculously yummy on much more than this salad alone, so pour it onto everything you make – especially if it seems weird!

SERVES 6 AS A MAIN, 8 AS A SIDE ————————————

1 Make the quinoa: rinse the quinoa well. In a small saucepan, combine the quinoa, water and salt. Bring to the boil, reduce the heat to low and cook, covered, for about 20 minutes until all the water has been absorbed and the quinoa grains are tender. Fluff with a fork.

2 Meanwhile, make the dressing: in a blender, combine the tahini, lime juice, olive oil, maple syrup, water, salt and mint leaves; blend on high until smooth and creamy. Season with more salt as needed. Set aside.

3 In a large bowl, combine the cabbages, kale, carrots and pepper.

QUINOA

85 g / 3 oz quinoa, soaked if possible

250 ml / 8 fl oz water

¼ tsp fine sea salt

MINTY TAHINI DRESSING

125 ml / 4 fl oz tahini

4 tbsp freshly squeezed lime juice

2 tbsp cold-pressed olive oil

1 tbsp pure maple syrup

185 ml / 6½ fl oz water

Pinch of sea salt, plus extra as needed

25 g / 1 oz fresh mint leaves

(recipe continues)

VEGETABLES

130 g / 4½ oz red cabbage, shredded

130 g / 4½ oz green cabbage, shredded

120 g / 4¼ oz kale, shredded

3 medium carrots, julienned

1 red pepper (stem, seeds and ribs removed), julienned

4 tbsp freshly squeezed lemon juice

1 tbsp cold-pressed olive oil

¼ tsp fine sea salt

100 g / 3½ oz unsweetened desiccated coconut

4 In a small bowl, whisk the lemon juice, olive oil and salt together and pour over the vegetables. Toss well and lightly massage the liquid into the kale and cabbage, then leave to marinate for 5–10 minutes.

5 Preheat a dry frying pan over a medium heat. When hot, toast the coconut, stirring frequently, for 2–3 minutes until golden brown and fragrant. Immediately remove the pan from the heat and set it aside.

6 Finish the salad: add the quinoa and coconut to the vegetable bowl. Toss well to combine. When ready to serve, dish out portions and allow guests to pour the dressing on their salads.

ROLLOVER **Make a double batch of the dressing for the Snappy Spring Salad (page 57).**

SPROUTED MUNG BEAN

and Mango Avocado Cups

For as long as I can remember, one of my mother's favourite snacks has been half an avocado scooped out and dressed with a little salt and lemon. When I was a kid the mere idea of this made me ill, but now the only thing I think could be better is the *entire* avocado. Very much inspired by my mum, this salad is a celebration of the steps I've taken towards a healthier life. Crunchy mung beansprouts, juicy sweet mango and lime combine to make a tropical-tasting treat that you could eat any time of the day – it actually makes a fantastic breakfast! This recipe calls for two large avocados to serve four people, but if you're anything like me, you'll go for a whole one too.

SERVES 2 AS A MAIN, 4 AS A SIDE ——————————————

1 Make the dressing: in a small bowl, whisk together the lime juice, olive oil and salt.

2 Prepare the salad: peel and cut the mango into bite-sized pieces. In a large bowl, combine the mango with the beansprouts, coriander, shallot and chilli flakes. Pour the dressing over the top and toss to coat. Season with salt.

3 Slice the avocados in half and remove the stones and a small portion of the flesh to create a space in each half for the filling.

4 Fold the extra avocado flesh into the salad, then fill each avocado with plenty of salad, letting it spill over the sides. Serve immediately.

ROLLOVER Make extra sprouted mung bean salad and serve it over cooked brown rice for a complete lunch the next day.

DRESSING

2 tbsp freshly squeezed lime juice

1 tbsp cold-pressed olive oil

2 pinches of sea salt flakes

SALAD

1 large ripe mango

180 g / 6 oz mung beansprouts (see Basic Sprouts, page 23)

20 g / ¾ oz chopped fresh coriander leaves and tender stems

1 shallot or ¼ red onion, very finely chopped

A few pinches of crushed chilli flakes

Fine sea salt

2 large ripe avocados

TERRIFIC TARRAGON
GREEN BEAN SALAD

85 g / 3 oz raw, unsalted pecans

400 g / 14 oz fresh green beans

175 g / 6 oz green peas, fresh or frozen

1 small red onion or a couple of shallots, very finely chopped

15 g / ½ oz chopped fresh tarragon leaves

Maple-mustard Dressing (recipe follows)

150 g / 5½ oz feta cheese (preferably goat's or sheep's), crumbled

Fine sea salt

1 tsp freshly ground black pepper

ROLLOVER If you have any extra tarragon, use it to replace the coriander in the Deep Detox Coriander, Spinach and Sweet Potato Soup (page 43).

This is one juicy jewel box of a salad! Sweet green peas, tender green beans, shallots, feta and pecans shine bright and beautifully together. Enjoy this in late spring and summer when beans and peas are fresh and in season. If you're not familiar with tarragon, it tastes like a combination of liquorice and basil with a pleasant lemony aftertaste. It also goes very well with other green foods, such as asparagus and artichokes, and it's especially delicious when combined with a strong mustard. If you want to make this ahead of time for a picnic, leave the dressing, cheese and nuts out until just before serving.

SERVES 2 AS A MAIN, 4 AS A SIDE

1 Start the salad: preheat the oven to 180°C / 350°F / Gas mark 4. Place the pecans on a rimmed baking sheet and toast for 5–7 minutes until fragrant. Remove from the oven and set aside.

2 Cook the vegetables: wash and trim the green beans. In a large pot fitted with a steamer basket, bring a small amount of water to the boil. Add the green beans and steam for 4–5 minutes until crisp-tender, being careful not to overcook. Remove the beans from the steamer basket and rinse them under cold water to halt the cooking process.

3 Return the steamer basket to the pot and add the peas to the basket. Steam the peas for 1–2 minutes until bright green and sweet. Drain and rinse them under cold water to halt the cooking process.

4 Finish the salad: place the green beans and peas in a large bowl with the red onion and tarragon. Pour the dressing over the top, toss to coat and sprinkle with the feta and pecans. Season with sea salt and the freshly ground black pepper.

MAPLE-MUSTARD DRESSING

MAKES A LITTLE MORE THAN 55 ML / 1¾ FL OZ

In a small bowl, whisk together the olive oil, maple syrup, mustard and vinegar. Season with salt and pepper. The dressing will keep, refrigerated in an airtight container, for up to 1 week.

3 tbsp cold-pressed olive oil

1½ tsp pure maple syrup

1 tbsp Dijon mustard

1 tbsp apple cider vinegar

Pinch of fine sea salt

Freshly ground black pepper

BALSAMIC-ROASTED PLUMS
with Spinach and Goat's Cheese

SALAD

4 medium plums (choose ones that are a little firmer than ripe)

1 tsp coconut oil or ghee, melted

1 tbsp balsamic vinegar

½ tsp freshly ground black pepper, plus extra to serve

100 g / 3½ oz baby spinach

100 g / 3½ oz soft goat's cheese

BALSAMIC DRESSING

2 tbsp cold-pressed olive oil

1½ tsp balsamic vinegar

1 tsp Dijon mustard

1 shallot, very finely chopped

Pinch of fine sea salt, plus extra to serve

This is a very simple and just plain yummy salad. Roasting the plums caramelizes and deepens the flavour of their sugars, while the balsamic vinegar adds a contrasting sour note. The salad would also be lovely topped with something crunchy, such as toasted almonds or walnuts. To make this dish even more substantial, add some cooked lentils and serve it with your favourite gluten-free bread or some crusty wholegrain sourdough.

SERVES 2 AS A MAIN, 4 AS A SIDE ————————————

1 Prepare the salad: preheat the oven to 180°C / 350°F / Gas mark 4.

2 Stone the plums and slice them into eighths. On a rimmed baking sheet lined with baking paper, toss the plum slices with the melted coconut oil, balsamic vinegar and black pepper. Roast for 15–20 minutes, turning once, until the plums are soft and caramelized. Leave to cool.

3 Meanwhile, wash the spinach and spin it dry. Transfer to a large bowl.

4 Make the dressing: in a small bowl, whisk together the olive oil, vinegar, mustard, shallot and salt. Pour the dressing over the spinach and toss to coat.

5 Finish the salad: scatter the plums over the dressed spinach and crumble the goat's cheese on top. Season with salt and pepper.

ROLLOVER Roast extra plums to use in the Copycat Couscous with Clementines (page 175) instead of the clementines.

EMERALD CITY SALAD

This is more of an idea than a recipe, and one that came to me while I was eating at a friend's place. We both love avocados, and before putting them in the salad she was serving, my friend cut them into rings. Rings! What a simple change to make, and what a beautiful impact it had – it was like eating a completely different vegetable. Inspired by this, I created a green-on-green salad with cucumber ribbons, lime juice, mint and chilli flakes for a result that sparkles and shimmers. You'll be off to see the Wizard with this easy, warm-weather dish!

SERVES 2 AS A MAIN, 4 AS A SIDE ──────────────────

2 ripe avocados

10 g / ¼ oz fresh mint leaves

1 large cucumber, preferably an English cucumber

Juice of 1 lime

1 tbsp cold-pressed olive oil

½ tsp crushed chilli flakes

Sea salt flakes

1 Slice the avocados crossways and around the stone into 0.5 cm/¼ in rings. Peel the skin off and place the flesh on a large serving platter. Stack the mint leaves, roll them into a cigar shape and slice them crossways to create ribbons.

2 Using a mandoline, cut the cucumber (including the skin) lengthways into long ribbons. Layer the cucumber with the avocado rings on the platter.

3 Pour the lime juice evenly over the top, drizzle with the olive oil and sprinkle with the chilli flakes, mint and sea salt. Serve immediately.

ROLLOVER Save any leftover salad for the Rainbow Hummus Bowl (page 74).

RAINBOW HUMMUS BOWL

75 ml / 2½ fl oz hummus of your choice

Fresh greens (such as spinach, rocket and romaine)

Handful of cooked beans or lentils

Handful of sprouts

Mix of chopped veggies (such as steamed green beans; roasted beetroot; raw pepper, carrots and/or avocado; and olives)

TO SERVE

Cold-pressed olive oil

Freshly squeezed lemon juice

Sea salt flakes

When I was in Los Angeles, I visited a brand-new raw-food restaurant that offered a falafel salad bowl – basically my dream come true on any menu. When the dish arrived, the vegetables themselves were lightly dressed, and the main attraction – a rich and delicious hummus – was generously smeared around the inside of the bowl so that each bite I took was adorned with it. Brilliant! I re-created it as soon as I got home, choosing an abundance of seasonal veggies prepared in a variety of ways, and using the hummus I had in the fridge at the time. This works any time of the year with any kind of hummus and is *the* perfect clean-out-the-fridge meal. Try it with one of the hummus recipes on pages 187–89.

SERVES 1 AS A MAIN ————————————————————

1 Smear the hummus around the inside of a single-serve salad bowl.

2 Add the greens, beans, sprouts and veggies and toss. Drizzle with olive oil and lemon juice and season with salt. Toss to coat.

ROLLOVER Sprout extra lentils to make the Sprouted Lentil Chilli (page 138).

TOMATOES

with Basil and Sunflower Meta Feta

SUNFLOWER META FETA

420 g / 15 oz raw, unsalted, shelled sunflower seeds, soaked for at least 2 hours, preferably overnight, drained and rinsed

1 tsp fine sea salt

1 large garlic clove

4 tbsp freshly squeezed lemon juice

5 tbsp water

CAPER DRESSING

3 tbsp cold-pressed olive oil

1½ tsp apple cider vinegar

1 tbsp pure maple syrup

2 pinches of fine sea salt, plus extra as needed

½ garlic clove, very finely chopped

2 tbsp capers, rinsed

4 medium tomatoes, in season if possible

Sea salt flakes

Freshly ground black pepper

Handful of fresh basil leaves

Tomatoes, basil and cheese is a well-loved, classic combination. But my curious heart has always wanted to make a vegan version. Introducing, 'meta feta': a spreadable sunflower seed 'cheese' with tons of flavour and versatility, perfect for salads, sandwiches and filling wraps.

This dish is delicious all year round, but because the main attraction is tomatoes you'll have the most delicious results in late summer, when they're at their peak of ripeness.

SERVES 2 AS A MAIN, 4 AS A SIDE

1 Make the Meta Feta: place the soaked and drained sunflower seeds, salt, garlic clove and lemon juice in a food processor. Pulse a few times to break down the seeds. Turn the motor on and drizzle the water into the machine in a thin stream as the mixture is processed. Stop a few times to scrape down the bowl. You're aiming for the texture of a thick, chunky hummus; add just enough additional water (up to 125 ml / 4 fl oz) to achieve that texture. Transfer the mixture to an airtight container and refrigerate for at least 30 minutes before using. This will keep in an airtight container in the fridge for up to 4 days.

2 Meanwhile, prepare the Caper Dressing: whisk together the olive oil, vinegar, maple syrup, salt, garlic and capers. Taste and adjust the seasonings, if necessary.

3 To serve, spread 125 g/ 4½ oz of the Meta Feta on a large platter or serving dish. Slice the tomatoes and lay them across the top. Season the salad with salt and pepper, sprinkle with the basil leaves and drizzle the Caper Dressing over the top.

ROLLOVER Use the extra Meta Feta from this recipe to make the Aubergine Cannelloni with Sunflower Feta and Toasted Garlic Tomato Sauce (page 114).

CELERY LEAF SALAD

with Balsamic Roasted Aubergine

Isn't it strange how we become accustomed to eating some parts of fruits and vegetables but not others? Celery leaves are the perfect example of this – we are so used to eating the stalk and tossing the rest away, but the leaves are supremely delicious. Waste not, want not! With an intense freshness and a pleasing bitterness, they pair with earthy flavours like aubergine and walnuts. This salad is a hearty dish and makes a wonderful lunch or light dinner.

SERVES 2 AS A MAIN, 4 AS A SIDE

4 tbsp balsamic vinegar

1 tbsp Dijon mustard

½ tsp crushed chilli flakes

¼ tsp fine sea salt

1 aubergine

75 g / 2¾ oz soft goat's cheese

40 g / 1½ oz raw, unsalted walnuts

60 g / 2¼ oz celery leaves

1 tbsp cold-pressed olive oil

1 Preheat the oven to 200°C / 400°F / Gas mark 6.

2 Whisk together the vinegar, mustard, chilli flakes and salt in a large bowl.

3 Slice the unpeeled aubergine into rounds about 1.3 cm / ½ in thick. Add to the bowl with the dressing and toss well to coat. Leave to marinate for 5 minutes. Place the aubergine slices on a baking sheet lined with baking paper and spoon some of the extra marinade on top, reserving the rest for the last step. Roast for 10 minutes, then flip and roast on the other side for a further 5–10 minutes until tender. Remove from the oven, crumble the goat's cheese over the top and grill for 2–3 minutes until golden.

4 Lower the oven temperature to 160°C / 325°F / Gas mark 3. Place the walnuts on another rimmed baking sheet and toast for 7–10 minutes until fragrant, watching them carefully so they do not burn. Remove the walnuts from the oven and roughly chop.

5 Wash and dry the celery leaves and place them in a medium bowl. Whisk the olive oil in with the remaining marinade. Pour over the celery leaves and toss to coat. Divide the celery leaves among plates, top with a few slices of aubergine and sprinkle the walnuts over the top.

SHINING SUMMER GRILLED COURGETTES AND CORN

with Basil

2 corn cobs

2 tsp coconut oil

2 courgettes

Sea salt flakes

Lemon Garlic Dressing
(page 54)

30 g / 1 oz pumpkin seeds

250 g / 9 oz cherry
tomatoes, whole or halved

Handful of fresh basil leaves

Crushed chilli flakes

ROLLOVER Grill 4 extra corn
cobs and use them in the
Cashew Corn Chowder with
Chipotle Oil (page 38). Double
up the Lemon Garlic Dressing
for the Roasted Sweet Potato
and Butter Beans on Massaged
Kale (page 54).

This is pure summer on a plate and the perfect example of how things that grow together taste amazing together! Although you can purchase these ingredients all year round, I highly recommend making this when the corn, courgettes, tomatoes and basil are fresh and bountiful and your grill is enjoying a healthy workout. To change things, try this salad with coriander or mint, use roasted hazelnuts or almonds and put it all on a bed of black beans for a heartier dish.

SERVES 2 AS A MAIN, 4 AS A SIDE ————————————————

1 Heat the grill to high. Husk the corn cobs and rub them with a little of the coconut oil. Place them on the grill and cook, turning every few minutes, until tender and bright yellow. Remove from the grill and leave them to cool. Cut off the corn kernels by standing each cob on its end in a shallow bowl and slicing downwards.

2 Slice the courgette lengthways into 0.5 cm / ¼ in thick pieces (not too thin or they will fall apart on the grill). Rub both sides of each slice with a little coconut oil and place on the grill. Cook, flipping once, until both sides are tender and lightly charred. Remove the courgettes from the grill and place in the bowl with the corn. Season with the sea salt flakes.

3 Pour half of the dressing over the corn and courgettes. Toss gently to coat and leave the vegetables to marinate for 5 minutes.

4 Preheat a small dry frying pan over a medium heat. When hot, toast the pumpkin seeds for 3–5 minutes, tossing frequently, until fragrant. Immediately remove the pan from the heat and set it aside.

5 Place the courgettes and corn on a large serving platter. Add the tomatoes and basil, pour the remaining dressing over the top and sprinkle with the pumpkin seeds and chilli flakes. Serve immediately.

ROCKET AND FIG SALAD
with Toasted Walnut Sauce

75 g / 2¾ oz rocket

3 large ripe figs

1 small red onion or shallot

Toasted Walnut Sauce, to serve (recipe follows)

Figs have the undeniable ability to turn any dish into a special one. The fact that they are only around for a few weeks a year makes me appreciate their uniqueness even more. This salad is an exceptional way to enjoy figs' fleeting moment, especially when paired with Toasted Walnut Sauce. The sauce's roasted-nut flavour and creamy texture will blow your mind! Here it combines perfectly with the mellow sweetness of figs, but try it on pasta and roasted veggies too.

SERVES 2 AS A MAIN, 4 AS A SIDE

1 Wash and dry the rocket.

2 Slice the figs into quarters. Slice the onions into thin rounds.

3 Divide all of the ingredients among plates. Drizzle with Toasted Walnut Sauce.

ROLLOVER Make extra Toasted Walnut Sauce for the Charred Cabbage with Apple and Toasted Walnut Sauce (page 179) or the Wild Rice, Roasted Carrot and Pomegranate Bold Bowl (page 147).

(recipe continues)

125 g / 4½ oz raw, unsalted walnuts

1 garlic clove

2 tbsp cold-pressed olive oil

4 tsp apple cider vinegar

2 tsp pure maple syrup or raw honey

2 generous pinches of fine sea salt, plus extra as needed

TOASTED WALNUT SAUCE

MAKES APPROXIMATELY 270 ML / 9½ FL OZ

1 Preheat the oven to 180°C / 350°F / Gas mark 4.

2 Spread the walnuts in a single layer on a rimmed baking sheet. Toast for 7–10 minutes until they are golden and fragrant, watching them carefully so they do not burn. Remove from the oven and cool slightly.

3 Add the toasted walnuts, garlic, olive oil, apple cider vinegar and maple syrup to a blender. Blend on high, adding up to 250 ml / 8 fl oz of water to thin the dressing as needed – you are looking for the consistency of melted ice cream. Season with salt. Store in an airtight glass container in the fridge for up to 5 days.

GINGER-PICKLED CARROT LENTIL SALAD

with Spiced Prunes and Dukkah

There is a wonderful balance of flavours going on here: the acidity of the carrots, the sweetness of the prunes and the deep spices from the dressing. You can make a couple of the elements ahead of time, and in fact, I recommend doing so. The carrots do not need a full twenty-four hours to pickle, but if you desire the full effect, it's the only way to go! The lentils can be cooked in advance and stored in the fridge so that all you have to do is toss everything together right before you serve. Most green lettuces will work here, but the softer, creamier Little Gem, and butter lettuces are my favourites.

SERVES 4 AS A MAIN, 6 AS A SIDE

1 In a small pot, cover the lentils with about 750 ml / 1¼ pints of water and bring to the boil over a high heat. Reduce the heat to low and simmer, covered, for 10–20 minutes until tender but not mushy, depending on whether or not you soaked them. Add the salt about 5 minutes before the lentils are done. Drain and lightly rinse the cooked lentils.

2 Make the dressing: whisk together the olive oil, lemon juice, cumin, cinnamon, coriander, paprika and salt. Pour half of the dressing over the lentils while they are still warm, and fold to coat.

3 Wash and dry the lettuce well. Separate the leaves and place in a large bowl or on a platter. Roughly chop the mint. Scatter the lentils over the lettuce, top with the pickled carrots, prunes and Dukkah and drizzle the remaining dressing over the top. Season with sea salt flakes. Sprinkle the salad with the mint leaves and serve.

200 g / 7 oz green lentils, soaked for 8 hours or overnight if possible

½ tsp fine sea salt

DRESSING

3 tbsp cold-pressed olive oil

4 tbsp freshly squeezed lemon juice

2 tsp ground cumin

1 tsp ground cinnamon

¼ tsp ground coriander

¼ tsp smoked hot paprika (ground chipotle would also work)

2 pinches of fine sea salt, plus extra as needed

1 small head of tender lettuce

5 g / ⅛ oz fresh mint leaves

Ginger-pickled Carrots (recipe follows)

85 g / 3 oz pitted prunes, chopped

3 tbsp Dukkah (page 26)

Sea salt flakes

(recipe continues)

GINGER-PICKLED CARROTS

MAKES ONE 1 LITRE / 35 FL OZ JAR

1 Scrub the carrots well. Using a vegetable peeler, slice the carrots lengthways into long, thin ribbons. Place the ribbons in a 1 litre / 35 fl oz glass container.

2 In a measuring jug, combine the vinegar, water, maple syrup, salt and ginger, and stir to dissolve the salt. Pour the brine over the carrots and add more water as needed to cover them completely. Seal the container and place the carrots in the fridge for at least 30 minutes, ideally 24 hours, before using. The carrots will keep in the fridge for up to 3 weeks.

ROLLOVER Use the Ginger-pickled Carrots in the Grilled Aubergine and Mushrooms with Saucy Almond Butter Noodles (page 133).

4 or 5 medium carrots

250 ml / 8 fl oz apple cider vinegar

250 ml / 8 fl oz water, plus extra as needed

1 tbsp pure maple syrup

1½ tsp fine sea salt

Small knob of fresh ginger (about 100 g / 3½ oz), peeled and sliced

CRAVEABLE CREAMY BRUSSELS SPROUT SLAW

with Apple and Toasted Almonds

SLAW

50 g / 1¾ oz raw almonds

30 g / 1 oz fresh flat-leaf parsley leaves and stems

250 g / 9 oz Brussels sprouts

1 apple

2 tsp freshly squeezed lemon juice

CREAMY MAPLE VINAIGRETTE

2 tbsp cold-pressed olive oil

4 tsp Dijon mustard

4 tsp apple cider vinegar

2 tsp pure maple syrup

65 g / 2¼ oz plain yogurt (preferably goat's or sheep's; optional)

2 pinches of fine sea salt

2 pinches of freshly ground black pepper, plus extra as needed

If any of you out there think that Brussels sprouts are absolutely uncraveable, this salad is here to show you otherwise! Simple, fresh and quite addictive, this dish is wonderful in the cooler months when Brussels and apples are at their peak.

The apple adds sweetness, the toasted almonds bring satisfying crunch and nuttiness and the parsley lends major brightness. Hazelnuts would be another delicious nut option here.

SERVES 2 AS A MAIN, 4 AS A SIDE ───────────────

1 Prepare the slaw: preheat the oven to 150°C / 300°F / Gas mark 2. Spread the almonds on a rimmed baking sheet in a single layer and roast for 20–25 minutes until fragrant and slightly darker in colour. (A good way to check is to bite one in half and check the colour in the centre – it should be golden.) Remove from the oven and leave to cool completely. Roughly chop the almonds and the parsley leaves, very finely chopping the stems.

2 While the almonds are roasting, wash and trim the Brussels sprouts, removing any damaged outer leaves. Slice them as thinly as possible using a knife or a food processor with the shredding attachment. Place in a large bowl.

3 Core and slice the apple into thin sections. In a small bowl, toss the apple sections with the lemon juice to prevent browning.

4 Make the dressing: whisk together the olive oil, mustard, apple cider vinegar, maple syrup, yogurt, salt and pepper.

5 Add the apples, almonds and parsley to the shredded Brussels, pour the dressing over the top, add a generous amount of black pepper and fold to combine.

ROLLOVER Roast double the almonds and use them for Twinkle, Twinkle, Jewelled Rice (page 176).

ROLLOVER Double the amount of cooked quinoa to use in the
Quinoa and Black Beans with Radish Coriander Salsa (page 106).

LEMONY RAW BEETROOT AND QUINOA SALAD

with Dill and Olives

Raw beetroot is one of my favourite foods. It is crisp yet tender, earthy and sweet. If you are one of the many people who have only tried cooked beetroot, be prepared to fall in love. The secret to the tastiest raw beetroot is to cut it very thinly. A mandoline is the best tool to create paper-thin slivers, but if you are confident with your knife skills, you can go the old-fashioned route. This salad is vegan, but if you are serving people who don't mind dairy, feta cheese is really lovely folded in.

SERVES 4 AS A MAIN, 6 AS A SIDE

190 g / 6½ oz quinoa, soaked if possible

415 ml / 14 fl oz water

¾ tsp fine sea salt

1 medium beetroot

1 tbsp freshly squeezed lemon juice

Lemon Garlic Dressing (page 54)

Zest of 1 lemon

50 g / 1¾ oz raw, unsalted pistachios

1 shallot, sliced

55 g / 2 oz chopped fresh dill

130 g / 4½ oz mixed green olives, with stones

1 Rinse the quinoa well. In a small saucepan, combine the quinoa, water and salt. Bring to the boil, reduce the heat to low and cook, covered, for about 20 minutes until all the water has been absorbed and the grains are tender. Fluff with a fork.

2 While the quinoa is cooking, peel the beetroot and thinly slice it with a mandoline. In a medium bowl, toss the beetroot slices with the freshly squeezed lemon juice. Set aside.

3 Pour half of the dressing and sprinkle the lemon zest over the cooked quinoa while it is still warm; toss to coat.

4 Preheat a small dry frying pan over a medium heat. When hot, toast the pistachios for about 5 minutes, stirring frequently, until fragrant. Immediately remove the pan from the heat, leave the nuts to cool and then roughly chop them.

5 Transfer the quinoa to a large bowl or serving platter. Add the sliced shallot and dill to the quinoa; fold to combine. Tuck the beetroot slices into the quinoa (if you toss them in, the quinoa will turn pink!), then add the olives and chopped pistachios. Drizzle the remaining dressing over the salad and season with salt.

nourishing
MAINS

PREVIOUS PAGE, from left to right: Massaged Kale, Feta and Pecans, page 96 / Mediterranean Broccoli and Chickpeas, page 97 / Spicy Cabbage and Black Beans, page 97

STUFFED SWEET POTATOES, 3 WAYS

If you read the *My New Roots* blog, you'll know just how obsessed I am with sweet potatoes. I love their versatility, incredible taste and astounding nutritional profile. They are very easy to serve roasted whole, sliced open and stuffed with whatever you're in the mood for. I get a lot of pleasure out of assemble-it-yourself food. Having a whole buffet of tasty things to mix and match at will makes me totally giddy. You can make one, two, or all three of these toppings for a buffet to suit any tastes, but I usually stick to just one on a weeknight. One stuffed potato makes a complete and satisfying lunch, dinner or even breakfast. Each of the toppings included here makes enough for about four medium sweet potatoes with extras – because you'll always want extra!

The skin of sweet potatoes is the most nutritious part of the vegetable, so try to find organic sweet potatoes if you can.

WHOLE ROASTED SWEET POTATOES

4 medium sweet potatoes

Cold-pressed olive oil, melted butter or ghee, for drizzling

Filling of your choice (pages 96 and 97)

SERVES 4 ————————————————————

1 Preheat the oven to 230°C / 450°F / Gas mark 8.

2 Scrub the sweet potatoes well, pierce them with a fork in a few places and set them on a rimmed baking sheet. Bake for 25–30 minutes, depending on the size of the potatoes. The potatoes are cooked when you can easily insert a sharp knife into the centre. Remove from the oven and slice each one lengthways, making sure not to cut them into two pieces. Drizzle with a little olive oil.

3 Serve the potatoes with one or more of the suggested fillings that follow. Undressed roasted sweet potatoes will keep in the fridge for up to 3 days. Reheat in a 200°C / 400°F / Gas mark 6 oven for 10 minutes.

(recipe continues)

MASSAGED KALE, FETA AND PECANS FILLING

50 g / 1¾ oz raw, unsalted pecans

90 g / 3¼ oz shredded curly kale

Juice of ½ lemon

2 tsp cold-pressed olive oil

2 pinches of fine sea salt, plus extra as needed

50 g / 1¾ oz crumbled feta

SERVES 4

1 Preheat the oven to 150°C / 300°F / Gas mark 2. Spread the pecans on a rimmed baking sheet in a single layer and roast them for 12–15 minutes until fragrant and slightly darker in colour. (A good way to check for doneness is to bite one in half and check the colour in the centre – it should be golden.) Remove from the oven and leave to cool completely. Roughly chop the pecans.

2 In a large bowl, combine the shredded kale, lemon juice, olive oil and salt. Using your hands, rub and squeeze the kale together as if you are giving it a massage, until the kale leaves are dark green and tender, about 2 minutes. Add the feta and pecans, toss everything to combine and season with salt.

MEDITERRANEAN BROCCOLI AND CHICKPEAS FILLING

SERVES 4

In a large bowl, whisk together the lemon zest and juice, olive oil, ½ teaspoon of salt and maple syrup. Add the broccoli, chickpeas, olives and pine nuts. Toss to combine and season with salt.

Zest of 1 lemon

Juice of ½ lemon

1 tbsp cold-pressed olive oil

½ tsp fine sea salt, plus extra as needed

1 tsp pure maple syrup or raw honey

160 g / 5¾ oz diced broccoli, both tops and stems

225 g / 8 oz (1 240 g / 8½ oz can) chickpeas, drained and rinsed

40 g / 1½ oz pitted olives (Kalamata is good choice)

25 g / 1 oz pine nuts

SPICY CABBAGE AND BLACK BEANS FILLING

SERVES 4

In a large bowl, combine the shredded cabbage, black beans, lime juice, olive oil, salt, coriander, spring onions and red chilli.

150 g / 5½ oz red cabbage, shredded

250 g / 9 oz (1 400 g / 14 oz can) black beans, drained and rinsed

Juice of 1 lime

1 tbsp cold-pressed olive oil

A few pinches of fine sea salt

15 g / ½ oz chopped fresh coriander leaves

2 spring onions, white and green parts, sliced

1 small red chilli (seeds removed), sliced (Serrano is a good choice)

FANTASTIC FALAFEL WAFFLES

400 g / 14 oz dried chickpeas

3 tbsp freshly squeezed lemon juice or apple cider vinegar

115 g / 4 oz gluten-free rolled oats

2 garlic cloves

15 g / ½ oz chopped fresh flat-leaf parsley

20 g / ¾ oz chopped fresh coriander leaves and tender stems

1½ tsp ground cumin

1½ tsp ground cinnamon

2 tsp ground coriander

1½ tsp fine sea salt

1 tsp freshly ground black pepper

Zest of 1 lemon

Coconut oil, for greasing the waffle iron

2 tbsp raw, unsalted sesame seeds

Spicy Lime Slaw (recipe follows)

Harissa Tahini Sauce (recipe follows)

Finely sliced red onion

Avocado slices

2 handfuls of your favourite sprouts

Crushed chilli flakes

Falafels sit at the top of my list for most attempts at a healthy makeover and at the bottom of my list for successful homemade meals. Why are they so darn delicious at a restaurant and so darn underwhelming at home? The secret, and most important aspect of awesome falafels, is to not cook your chickpeas. Nope. Use raw chickpeas and soak them for twenty-four hours (so make sure to start this recipe a day ahead of time).

MAKES 10–12 WAFFLES

1 In a large bowl, cover the chickpeas with plenty of water and 2 tablespoons of the lemon juice. Leave to soak for 24 hours, then drain and rinse them very well. Set aside.

2 In a food processor, pulse the oats until a roughly textured flour forms. Transfer the oat flour to a bowl and set aside. Without cleaning the food processor, add the garlic and pulse to very finely chop. Add the chickpeas, chopped herbs, spices, salt, pepper, lemon zest and the remaining tablespoon of lemon juice. Pulse until the chickpeas are very finely chopped but not pasty. Transfer the contents to a large mixing bowl.

3 Add the oat flour to the chickpea mixture and mix well, then add 4 tablespoons of water a spoonful at a time, stirring in between additions, until the dough holds together well when pressed.

4 Heat a waffle iron to medium-high and preheat the oven to 95°C / 200°F / lowest possible gas mark. Brush the iron with a little coconut oil. Divide the falafel dough into 10–12 equal portions, gently packing each portion so that it holds together well, especially around the edges. Flatten out a portion and press it into the hot waffle iron with the back of a spatula, then lower the lid and cook the falafel until it is golden brown and crisp, anywhere from 5–10 minutes, depending on your iron. Transfer the falafel from the waffle iron to a baking paper-lined baking sheet and keep it in the warm oven until ready to serve. Repeat with the remaining portions, brushing the iron with more coconut oil, if necessary.

5 While the waffles are cooking, heat a dry frying pan over a medium heat. Add the sesame seeds and toast, stirring frequently for 3–4 minutes, until fragrant and just beginning to pop. Remove from the heat.

6 Serve the hot falafel waffles with the Spicy Lime Slaw, Harissa Tahini Sauce, toasted sesame seeds, red onion, avocado, sprouts, chilli flakes and anything else you fancy!

SPICY LIME SLAW

MAKES APPROXIMATELY 300 G / 10½ OZ

In a large bowl, combine the cabbage, salt and lime juice. Massage the cabbage for about a minute until it begins to wilt. Drizzle with the olive oil and maple syrup. Season with more salt, as liked, and fold in the herbs and chilli. Store any leftovers in an airtight container in the fridge for up to 2 days.

300 g / 10½ oz finely shredded red cabbage

½ tsp fine sea salt, plus extra as needed

1½ tsp freshly squeezed lime juice

1 tbsp cold-pressed olive oil

1 tsp pure maple syrup or raw honey, plus extra as needed

Handful of chopped fresh flat-leaf parsley or fresh coriander leaves and tender stems, or both

1 small red chilli (seeds removed), sliced (Serrano is a good choice)

HARISSA TAHINI SAUCE

MAKES ABOUT 250 ML / 8 FL OZ

In a blender, combine the tahini, garlic, lemon juice, olive oil, harissa paste, maple syrup and a pinch of salt. Blend on high until smooth and creamy, adding approximately 125 ml / 4 fl oz of water to thin the sauce as desired. The sauce will keep in an airtight container in the fridge for up to 1 week.

5 tbsp tahini

1 large garlic clove, very finely chopped

2 tbsp freshly squeezed lemon juice

1 tbsp cold-pressed olive oil

2 tsp gluten-free harissa paste (available at Middle Eastern grocery stores)

1 tsp pure maple syrup or raw honey

Fine sea salt

RUN WILD SUMMER ROLLS

Whether you're having friends over for dinner or you're just trying to impress yourself, these fresh and lively summer rolls will do the trick. Although there is a bit of prep involved, they aren't complicated, and once all the chopping is complete, they assemble really quickly. This recipe uses three different building blocks that you can make ahead or take from other recipes – the Radish Coriander Salsa, the Spicy Lime Slaw and the Almond Butter Sauce – but you can really use any number of fresh salads, noodles, veggies and dipping sauces. The Spicy Tahini Ginger Sauce (page 104) is particularly good with these rolls. Let your imagination run wild and get rolling!

SERVES 2 AS A MAIN (4 ROLLS PER PERSON) ————————

1 Preheat a small dry frying pan over a medium heat. When hot, toast the sesame seeds, stirring frequently, for 2–3 minutes until fragrant. Remove the pan from the heat and set aside.

2 Fill a shallow dish a little larger than the rice paper wraps with room-temperature water. Place one wrap in the water until it becomes soft and pliable but not completely limp, about 1 minute.

3 Transfer the wrap to a clean work surface and place a little salsa, slaw, carrot, avocado, sprouts, a sprinkling of sesame seeds and a few mint leaves in the centre, plus a drizzle of sauce (avoid the temptation to overstuff with fillings).

4 Fold the top half of the wrap over the fillings. Then fold in both sides. Lastly, fold the bottom up to seal. If the rice paper breaks or it seems like the whole thing is going to fall apart (don't worry, it does sometimes), you can simply reinforce the roll by wrapping it in another sheet of soaked rice paper. Repeat steps 2–4 to make 7 more rolls. Serve immediately with the remaining sauce.

40 g / 1½ oz raw, unsalted sesame seeds

8 rice paper wraps

Radish Coriander Salsa (page 108)

Spicy Lime Slaw (page 99)

1 medium carrot, julienned

1 ripe avocado, sliced

50 g / 1¾ oz sprouts

Handful of fresh mint leaves

Almond Butter Sauce (page 135)

ROLLOVER **Make a double batch of the Radish Coriander Salsa for the Quinoa and Black Beans with Radish Coriander Salsa (page 106).**

SURPRISING SUNFLOWER SEED RISOTTO

350 g / 12 oz raw, unsalted, shelled sunflower seeds

2 tbsp fine sea salt, plus extra as needed

250 ml / 8 fl oz water

1 tbsp coconut oil or ghee

2 medium yellow onions, finely diced

5 garlic cloves, very finely chopped

500 ml / 18 fl oz vegetable stock

450 g / 1 lb (1 bunch) asparagus, stems removed, roughly chopped

150 g / 5½ oz shelled fresh green peas

TO SERVE

Cold-pressed olive oil

Small handful of chopped fresh flat-leaf parsley

Sea salt flakes

Lemon wedges

To say that this recipe is *totally* surprising would be an understatement. Rice-less risotto made from sunflower seeds?! It may just be the wildest thing I've ever cooked – successfully, anyway. The sunflower seeds are tender and chewy, with just the slightest bit of toothiness – not unlike rice cooked al dente. It's remarkably simple to make with just a few common ingredients, truly delicious, and deeply satisfying. The seeds create a foundation you can build upon no matter what time of year it is, so feel free to make it with any seasonal vegetables. I chose to go the spring route with peas and asparagus, but this would be equally as lovely with sautéed mushrooms, roasted root vegetables, pumpkin or squash.

SERVES 4 ───────────────────

1 Soak the sunflower seeds overnight or all day with the sea salt in a large bowl of filtered water.

2 Drain and rinse the sunflower seeds. In a blender, add 135 g / 4¾ oz of the soaked seeds and the water and blend on high until smooth. Set aside.

3 In a large stockpot or pan, melt the coconut oil over a medium-high heat. Add the onions and a pinch of sea salt, stir to coat and cook for 5–7 minutes until translucent. Add the garlic and cook for a further 2 minutes. Add the remaining whole sunflower seeds and just enough of the stock to cover the seeds. Reduce the heat to low and simmer, covered, for 20–30 minutes. The seeds are done when they are al dente, tender with only the slightest crunch still left in them. If there seems to be a lot of liquid left in the pot, leave it to simmer uncovered for a further 5 minutes until the excess liquid evaporates.

4 Stir in the sunflower cream from the blender and heat it gently. Season with salt.

5 Bring a pot of salted water to the boil. Add the asparagus, reduce the heat to low and simmer for about 2 minutes, then add the peas and simmer for a further 2 minutes, being careful not to overcook them. Drain and rinse the vegetables with cold water.

6 To serve, place about a quarter of the risotto on each plate, then top with the vegetables. Drizzle with olive oil, top with parsley and a sprinkling of sea salt flakes and serve with lemon wedges.

COOL IT NOODLE SALAD

with Radishes and Peas

SPICY TAHINI GINGER SAUCE

125 ml / 4 fl oz tahini

2 tbsp grated peeled fresh ginger

2 tbsp gluten-free tamari or soy sauce

2 tsp pure maple syrup or raw honey

1 tbsp freshly squeezed lime juice

125 ml / 4 fl oz water

NOODLE SALAD

250 g / 9 oz dried wholegrain noodles or pasta

150 g / 5½ oz green peas, fresh or frozen

2 medium carrots, julienned

200 g / 7 oz (1 small bunch) radishes, sliced

15 g / ½ oz chopped fresh coriander, to garnish

Sesame Salt, to serve (page 157)

When summer heats up, heaven bless the cold noodle salad! I like to make a big batch of this and keep it in the fridge for when hunger strikes and the last thing I want to do is turn on the hob to boil water. (Tip: make this in the morning!) Any vegetables work well here, and you can easily adapt this for any time of the year. . . you could even serve it hot.

Although I would traditionally use rice noodles for this dish, it can be difficult to find brown rice noodles at mainstream supermarkets, so I opt for the wholegrain pasta instead. The sauce is a riff on peanut sauce, with ginger, lime and maple syrup for sweetness. Although you can substitute peanut butter for the tahini, the latter is a healthier option.

SERVES 4

1 Make the sauce: place the tahini, ginger, tamari, maple syrup, lime juice and the water in a blender and blend on high until smooth and creamy. Taste and adjust the seasonings, if necessary. Set aside.

2 Prepare the noodle salad: bring a pot of heavily salted water to the boil. Add the pasta and cook until just less than al dente, according to the packet instructions. Add the peas to the boiling water, remove from the heat and leave to stand for 1 minute. Drain and rinse with cold water.

3 In a large serving bowl, toss the pasta and peas with the carrots and radishes. Pour about three-quarters of the sauce over the top and toss to combine. Divide the noodles among four bowls and garnish with coriander, more sauce if liked and Sesame Salt.

ROLLOVER Make double the Spicy Tahini Ginger Sauce for the Run Wild Summer Rolls (page 101).

QUINOA AND BLACK BEANS

with Radish Coriander Salsa

6 large carrots

2 garlic cloves

1 tbsp coconut oil or ghee, melted

2 pinches plus ¼ tsp fine sea salt

85 g / 3 oz quinoa, soaked if possible

250 ml / 8 fl oz water

250 g / 9 oz (1 400 g / 14 oz can) cooked black beans, drained and rinsed

1 tbsp cold-pressed olive oil

Juice of 1 lime

1 tsp crushed chilli flakes

Radish Coriander Salsa (recipe follows)

Hot sauce, to serve (optional)

This one-bowl wonder combines southwestern flavours with the surprising freshness and crunch of radishes bathed in lime and coriander. This salsa can be made a day in advance, but it should be dressed just before serving. It is delicious folded into smashed avocado for a twist on guacamole, or even paired with hummus in a wrap or pitta. You'll notice it appears several times in the book since it is easy to make and incredibly versatile. This is a great dish to whip up when you have leftover quinoa and black beans. Serve it with your favourite hot sauce for an extra kick!

SERVES 4 ──────────────────────────────

1 Preheat the oven to 200°C / 400°F / Gas mark 6. Scrub the carrots and slice them on the diagonal, about 1.3 cm / ½ in thick. Very finely chop the garlic. Place the carrots and garlic in a single layer on a rimmed baking sheet, drizzle with the coconut oil and toss to coat. Roast for about 20 minutes until tender and blistered. Remove them from the oven, season with the 2 pinches of salt and set aside.

2 Meanwhile, cook the quinoa. Rinse the grains and drain well. Place the quinoa in a small saucepan with the water and ¼ teaspoon of salt. Bring to the boil, reduce the heat to low and cook, covered, for about 20 minutes until all the water has been absorbed and the grains are tender.

3 In a large serving dish, combine the cooked quinoa and black beans with the olive oil and lime juice. Toss and season with more salt and the chilli flakes. Fold in the carrots and garlic.

(recipe continues)

4 Place a large mound of the Radish Coriander Salsa on top of the salad, or allow your guests to help themselves. Garnish with more chilli flakes and hot sauce, if liked.

ROLLOVER Cook double the black beans to use in a Stuffed Sweet Potato (page 95).

225 g / 8 oz radishes, finely diced

1½ tsp very finely chopped red onion or shallot

15 g / ½ oz chopped fresh coriander

2–3 tsp very finely chopped red chilli (Serrano is a good choice)

DRESSING

3 tbsp freshly squeezed lime juice

3 tbsp cold-pressed olive oil

1 tbsp pure maple syrup

2 pinches of fine sea salt, plus extra as needed

RADISH CORIANDER SALSA

MAKES ABOUT 250 ML / 8 FL OZ

1 In a medium bowl, combine the radishes, onion, coriander and chilli.

2 Make the dressing: in a small bowl, whisk together the lime juice, olive oil, maple syrup and salt. Just before serving, pour the dressing over the vegetables, fold to combine and season with more salt as liked.

CHICKPEA CURRY SALAD SANDWICH

It's time to make a case for mayonnaise. I know what you're thinking: how could a nutritionist be championing such an unhealthy food?! But let's look at what mayo actually is: it's primarily just oil and an egg. Do you think oil and eggs are unhealthy? If they are of high quality, then I certainly don't! The nutritional benefits and flavour of your mayonnaise are 100 per cent dependent on the quality of the things you make it with, and making mayo at home allows you to control these things. Use only the highest-quality cold-pressed olive oil here (for tips on how to buy olive oil, see page 230), and choose the best eggs you can find.

Needing a seriously awesome vehicle for this mayo, and inspired by the chicken salad sandwiches of my youth, I came up with this vegetarian version that will knock your socks off.

MAKES 8–10 SANDWICHES

1 Make the dressing: in a small bowl, whisk together the mayonnaise, curry powder, lemon juice and salt and pepper. Season with more salt, if necessary.

2 Make the salad: in a food processor, pulse the chickpeas to roughly chop them – do not overprocess or you'll end up with chickpea purée. You can also do this step by hand.

3 Chop the pecans and raisins, then dice the celery and spring onions.

4 In a large bowl, combine the chopped chickpeas with the dressing. Add the pecans, raisins, celery and onions and fold to combine. Season with salt. Enjoy the salad on bread with lettuce and onion slices, if liked.

CURRY DRESSING

6 tbsp Divine and Foolproof Mayonnaise (recipe follows)

1 tbsp curry powder

1½ tsp freshly squeezed lemon juice

Fine sea salt and freshly ground pepper

SALAD

450 g / 1 lb (2 400 g / 14 oz cans) cooked chickpeas, drained and rinsed

30 g / 1 oz raw pecans

3 tbsp raisins

1 celery stick

2 spring onions

TO SERVE

6–8 slices of wholegrain bread (sourdough if possible)

Crisp lettuce or sprouts

Sliced red onion or shallots (optional)

(recipe continues)

DIVINE AND FOOLPROOF MAYONNAISE

MAKES ABOUT 250 ML / 8 FL OZ

1 egg, at room temperature

1 tsp Dijon mustard

2 pinches of fine sea salt

1 tbsp freshly squeezed
lemon juice

175 ml / 6 fl oz cold-pressed
olive oil

1 Crack the egg into the bottom of a wide-mouth jar. Add the mustard, salt, lemon juice and olive oil.

2 Cover the entire egg with the head of an immersion blender (*Note:* this will not work with an upright blender) and blend on medium speed. When you can see that the mixture has thickened and turned white at the bottom of the jar, slowly move the blender up, waiting for the oil to be incorporated as you go, until you get the texture of mayonnaise.

3 Use immediately; refrigerate leftovers in an airtight jar for up to 1 month. The mayonnaise will thicken slightly once it has cooled in the fridge.

SMOKED LENTIL TACOS

with Pico de Gallo

PICO DE GALLO

250 g / 9 oz diced cherry tomatoes

65 g / 2¼ oz very finely chopped white onion

1 tsp very finely chopped red chilli (Serrano is a good choice)

2 tbsp lime juice

7 g / ¼ oz chopped fresh coriander leaves and tender stems

Fine sea salt

FILLING

210 g / 7½ oz green lentils, soaked for 8 hours or up to overnight, if possible

1 tbsp coconut oil

3 small yellow onions, sliced

1 tsp fine sea salt

1 large garlic clove, very finely chopped

35 g / 1¼ oz sun-dried tomatoes, chopped

1 tsp smoked hot paprika

1½ tsp dried oregano

2 tsp gluten-free tamari or soy sauce

TO SERVE

6 corn tortillas

Spicy Lime Slaw (page 99)

1 ripe avocado, sliced

Hot sauce (optional)

I haven't eaten any kind of meat in a very long time, but taking my first bite of these insanely tasty tacos made me feel as if I were. You see, meat contains ample amounts of glutamate, an amino acid that is responsible for umami, the taste of yummy savoury-ness that helps us feel satisfied. In an attempt to make tacos that lacked for nothing, I knew I had to infuse a ton of mouthwatering flavours into the lentils, so I used my secret weapons: sun-dried tomatoes, tamari and caramelized onions. The smokiness that we often associate with meat comes from the addition of hot smoked paprika – a genius spice to have in your meat-free arsenal.

MAKES 6 TACOS

1 Make the Pico de Gallo: in a small bowl, combine the cherry tomatoes, onion, chilli, lime juice and coriander. Season with salt and set aside.

2 Prepare the filling: in a stockpot or pan, combine the lentils and enough water to cover them. Bring to the boil, reduce the heat to low and cook, covered, for about 20 minutes until tender. Drain and rinse well.

3 Meanwhile, in a frying pan, melt the coconut oil over a medium-high heat. Add the onions and salt, stir to coat and cook for about 10 minutes until the onions soften and begin to slightly caramelize. Add the garlic, sun-dried tomatoes, paprika, oregano and tamari. Stir to coat, adding a little water if the pot is too dry. Cook for 2–3 minutes until fragrant, then add the lentils and stir well to incorporate. Taste and season with salt, if necessary, and remove from the heat.

4 To assemble, divide the smoky lentil mixture among the tortillas, followed by the slaw and Pico de Gallo. Add the avocado and hot sauce, if liked.

ROLLOVER Make a double batch of Pico de Gallo and use it in the Quinoa and Black Beans with Radish Coriander Salsa (page 106) instead of the Radish Coriander Salsa.

AUBERGINE CANNELLONI

with Sunflower Feta and Toasted Garlic Tomato Sauce

2 large aubergines

1 tsp coconut oil

½ tsp fine sea salt

TOASTED GARLIC TOMATO SAUCE

4 tbsp cold-pressed olive oil, plus extra for drizzling

3 garlic cloves, very finely chopped

½–1 tsp crushed chilli flakes, plus extra to garnish (optional)

½ tsp fine sea salt

1 800 g / 28 oz can chopped tomatoes

FILLING

80 g / 3 oz Kalamata olives

Handful of fresh basil leaves

250 g / 9 oz Sunflower Meta Feta (page 76)

Fine sea salt

ROLLOVER Make enough meta feta to use in the Tomatoes with Basil and Sunflower Meta Feta (page 76).

This recipe for cannelloni skips the pasta and uses roasted aubergine slices instead, making my version lighter and also grain-free. The filling is made from sunflower feta mixed with basil and olives, so it is vegan as well as gluten-free; it's also super bright and totally satisfying. The sunflower feta recipe makes more than you'll need here, but you can use it for many things, so make a big batch and get creative!

SERVES 4 ───────────────────────────

1 Preheat the oven to 200°C / 400°F / Gas mark 6.

2 Slice the aubergines lengthways into long, thin strips (about 0.5 cm / ¼ in; you should end up with at least 12 slices). Rub the aubergine slices with the coconut oil and sprinkle with the sea salt. Lay them on a rimmed baking sheet lined with baking paper.

3 Roast the aubergine slices for 10 minutes, flip them, then roast for a further 5–10 minutes until soft and browned. Remove from the oven and leave to cool slightly.

4 Meanwhile, make the sauce: in a medium saucepan, warm the olive oil over a low heat. Add the garlic and leave to lightly simmer until golden, about 1 minute, being careful not to let the oil smoke or the garlic burn. Add the chilli flakes, salt and tomatoes; stir well. Taste and adjust the seasonings, if necessary. Remove from the heat and set aside, covered, until ready to serve.

5 Make the filling: remove the stones from the olives and roughly chop. Tear the basil leaves. Mix together the meta feta, olives and basil. Season with salt.

6 Place about 2 tablespoons of the filling at one end of an aubergine slice. Roll it up and place it back on the baking sheet, seam-side down. Repeat with the remaining filling and slices. Return the aubergine to the oven to warm, if liked.

7 To serve, ladle one-quarter of the sauce onto each plate. Top with at least 3 aubergine rolls, drizzle with olive oil and sprinkle with extra chilli flakes, if liked.

WARMING CHICKPEA MUSHROOM RAGOUT

with Crispy Sage

Ragout is just a fancy French word for 'stew', so there's no need to be intimidated by this dish at all. In fact, its ingredients are wholeheartedly humble, and I love tucking into this simple meal on a cold winter's night; it'll warm you from head to toe. Or serve it with a poached egg on top for a lovely weekend breakfast. As much as I like eating this ragout on brown rice, polenta is another wonderful option. Also, it's important not to wash the mushrooms – they will absorb water, and their flavour will be diluted. Instead, brush them clean with damp kitchen towel to remove any soil or debris.

SERVES 3–4

1 In a medium saucepan with a tight-fitting lid, combine the rice, water and ¾ teaspoon of the salt. Bring to the boil, reduce the heat to low and simmer, covered, for 45–50 minutes until the rice is tender and has absorbed the water. If the rice is not yet cooked and needs more water, add about 4 tablespoons of water and continue cooking.

2 Meanwhile, chop the onions and very finely chop the garlic. Melt 1 tablespoon of the coconut oil in a large stockpot or pan over a medium heat. Add the onions and the remaining teaspoon of salt, stir to coat and cook for about 10 minutes until the onions soften and begin to slightly caramelize (add a little stock if the pot becomes too dry). Add the garlic, chopped sage, rosemary, thyme and mushrooms. Turn the heat to high and cook, stirring every so often, for about 10 minutes until the mushrooms have released their liquid and softened. Add the remaining stock, milk, vinegar, black pepper and chickpeas. Lower the heat and simmer until the liquid has reduced and thickened slightly.

200 g / 7 oz brown rice

500 ml / 18 fl oz water

1¾ tsp fine sea salt, plus extra for sprinkling

3 medium yellow onions

3 garlic cloves

2 tbsp coconut oil or ghee

125 ml / 4 fl oz vegetable stock

10 g / ¼ oz fresh sage leaves, roughly chopped, plus 16 extra for frying

1½ tsp dried rosemary

1½ tsp dried thyme

400 g / 14 oz chestnut mushrooms, sliced into quarters

125 ml / 4 fl oz plant-based milk of your choice

1 tbsp balsamic vinegar

1 tsp freshly ground black pepper

225 g / 8 oz (1 240 g / 8½ oz can) cooked chickpeas, drained and rinsed

1½ tsp freshly squeezed lemon juice

50 g / 1¾ oz spinach leaves

(recipe continues)

3 In a small frying pan, melt the remaining tablespoon of coconut oil over a medium-high heat. When hot, add 6–8 whole sage leaves at a time and fry them for 10–15 seconds. Using a fork, transfer the leaves to kitchen towel and immediately sprinkle with sea salt. Repeat with the remaining leaves.

4 Remove the ragout from the heat and stir in the lemon juice and spinach leaves just before serving over the rice. Top each plate with 4 crispy sage leaves.

ROLLOVER Cook double the brown rice to make a meal out of the Kale, Mushrooms and Walnuts with Pecorino (page 158).

PORTOBELLO PIZZAS

Although I am not emotionally equipped to live in a world without traditional pizza, this is a really great alternative if you are looking to fill up on more vegetables instead of grains or starches. Marinated mushrooms create a mega-flavoured base for caramelized onions, garlicky spinach and caper-spiked tomatoes. Although there is a generous cheese mountain on top of these guys, they are delicious without it, if you want the dish to be vegan. Although the recipe makes one mushroom per person, if you have a big appetite (or you are as gluttonous as I am), you may want to make extra!

MAKES 6 PIZZAS

1 Using a clean, damp kitchen towel, brush the mushroom caps well, carefully removing any dirt. Remove the stems, roughly chop them and set aside.

2 In a large resealable plastic bag, combine the vinegar, thyme, oregano, rosemary, 3 of the very finely chopped garlic cloves and ½ teaspoon of the salt, smooshing and sloshing the mixture a bit to incorporate. Place the whole mushroom caps in the bag, seal it up, roll the contents around to coat them with the marinade and leave in the fridge for a minimum of 30 minutes, or up to 3 hours. If you think of it, take the bag out from time to time and roll it around to ensure that the mushrooms are well covered with the marinade.

3 In a large frying pan, melt the coconut oil over a medium-high heat. Add the onions, chopped mushroom stems and the remaining ½ teaspoon of salt and toss to coat. Cook, stirring frequently, for about 20 minutes until the onions soften and are fully caramelized. Add a little water to the pan if it becomes dry.

6 large portobello mushrooms

4 tbsp balsamic vinegar

1½ tsp dried thyme

1½ tsp dried oregano

1½ tsp dried rosemary

4 garlic cloves, very finely chopped

1 tsp fine sea salt

1 tbsp coconut oil or ghee

3 medium yellow onions, sliced

100 g / 3½ oz baby spinach leaves

225 g / 8 oz tomatoes

50 g / 1¾ oz capers, rinsed

Freshly ground black pepper

Pecorino Romano, to garnish (optional; Parmesan will also work)

Handful of fresh basil leaves, to garnish (optional)

(recipe continues)

4 Transfer the caramelized onions to a bowl without cleaning the pan. Add the remaining very finely chopped garlic clove and the spinach to the pan with a small splash of water. Increase the heat to high and wilt the spinach, stirring frequently, for 1–2 minutes until it is dark green and soft, being careful not to overcook.

5 Chop the tomatoes and combine them with the capers and black pepper in a small bowl.

6 Preheat the oven to 200°C / 400°F / Gas mark 6. Assemble the mushroom caps by placing them top-side down on a rimmed baking sheet lined with baking paper. Spoon about one-sixth of the caramelized onions on to each mushroom. Top each with some wilted spinach, followed by the tomato-caper mixture. You can add some grated cheese at this point if you like, or wait until after the pizzas have come out of the oven.

7 Bake for 15–20 minutes until the mushrooms are heated through. Grate the cheese over top and garnish with the basil if liked. Serve hot.

BUTTERNUT SQUASH AND SAGE OVEN RISOTTO

2 tbsp ghee or coconut oil (preferably ghee)

2 medium yellow onions, finely diced

1 tsp fine sea salt

1.2–1.7 litres / 2–3 pints vegetable stock

4 garlic cloves

15 fresh sage leaves, sliced

1 kg / 2 lb 4 oz butternut squash, peeled and chopped into 1.3 cm / ½ in cubes

500 g / 1 lb 2 oz short-grain brown rice, soaked overnight if possible

1 rind of Pecorino Romano

Cold-pressed olive oil, to serve

Freshly grated Pecorino Romano or Parmesan, to serve (optional)

ROLLOVER Save extra sage for the Warming Chickpea Mushroom Ragout with Crispy Sage (page 117).

Risotto intimidates a lot of people, but I think this comes from the sheer notion of commitment: having to stand by the hob for some time, stir the pot constantly, add stock at *just* the right moment and make sure the rice is neither under- nor overcooked but perfectly al dente. This oven method eliminates pretty much all of that.

Short-grain brown rice is the best rice to use here because it is starchier than long-grain brown rice, which helps to create a creamy consistency. The incredible depth of flavour comes from using a cheese rind. I always save my rinds in the freezer until an occasion such as this comes along. You will not believe how it permeates the entire dish, which means that you need to add very little extra cheese at the end to achieve the deep umami taste we all crave.

SERVES 4–6

1 Preheat the oven to 220°C / 425°F / Gas mark 7.

2 In a large ovenproof pot fitted with a lid, melt the ghee over a medium heat. Add the onions and salt and sauté for 10 minutes until translucent and slightly caramelized, adding a little stock if the pot becomes too dry. Add the garlic and sage and cook for 2 minutes until fragrant.

3 Add the butternut squash, rice, 1.2 litres / 2 pints of stock and the cheese rind to the pot. Stir well, cover the pot and bake for 20 minutes. Remove from the oven, stir once and check the liquid levels. If you think that there is not enough stock, add 250 ml / 8 fl oz or so, then cover the pot and put it back in the oven, checking every 15 minutes or so until the rice is tender. It should cook for about 60 minutes if your rice has been soaked, up to 90 minutes if you start with dry rice.

4 Serve hot with a drizzle of olive oil and extra Pecorino Romano grated over the top, if liked.

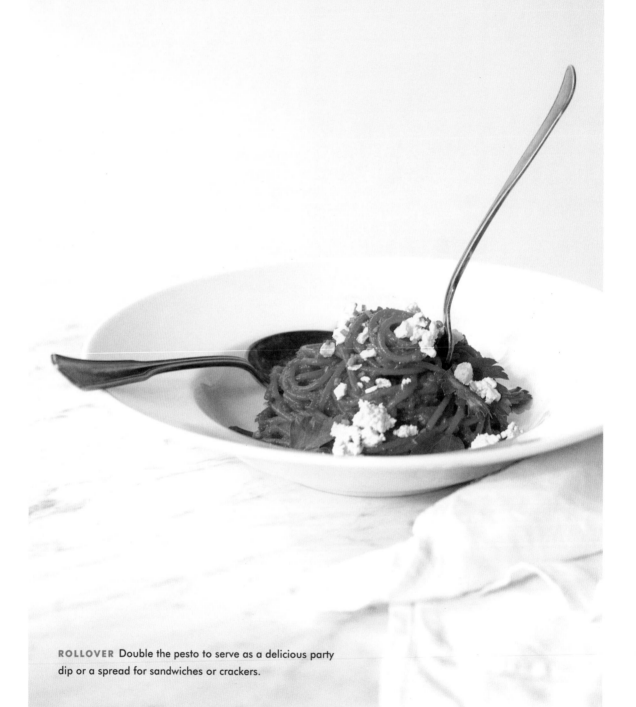

ROLLOVER Double the pesto to serve as a delicious party dip or a spread for sandwiches or crackers.

VIBRANT PINK PESTO PASTA

Vibrant food is healthy food! Deep pigments signal powerful nutrients, and there is something so alluring about the rich magenta hue of this pasta dish. The pesto uses roasted beetroot to attain its bright-pink pigment and cleverly dyes the pasta that it touches, creating a unique and totally unexpected visual. Choose wholegrain pasta for this recipe, and don't worry if it is naturally dark in colour; the pesto will undoubtedly shine through – it's powerful stuff! The goat's cheese is an optional topping, but it adds a gorgeous, creamy texture and salty counterpoint to the earthy-sweet pesto. If you don't have parsley on hand, basil or mint would also be delicious.

SERVES 4–6

1 Preheat the oven to 200°C / 400°F / Gas mark 6. Wrap the beetroot in foil and roast for 40–60 minutes until tender. Remove the beetroot from the oven, unwrap the foil and cool slightly before slipping off the skins.

2 While the beetroot is roasting, heat a large frying pan over a medium heat. Add the pumpkin seeds and lightly toast, stirring occasionally, for 3–5 minutes until fragrant. Remove from the heat and set aside.

3 In a food processor, pulse the garlic until very finely chopped. Roughly chop the beetroot and add it to the processor along with the pumpkin seeds, lemon juice, olive oil and salt, and process until relatively smooth. Taste and add more salt and lemon juice as needed.

4 Fill a large pot with water and bring to the boil. Add salt and the pasta and cook until al dente, according to the packet instructions. Drain, place the pasta back in the pot and drizzle with olive oil. Stir in the pesto.

5 To serve, divide the cooked pasta among individual plates, crumble the cheese on top, sprinkle with parsley and season with salt. Garnish with extra olive oil, if liked.

PESTO

450 g / 1 lb red beetroot

50 g / 1¾ oz raw, unsalted pumpkin seeds

2 garlic cloves

1½ tsp freshly squeezed lemon juice, plus extra as needed

3 tbsp cold-pressed olive oil

½ tsp fine sea salt, plus extra as needed

PASTA

Fine sea salt

600 g / 1 lb 5 oz dried wholegrain pasta of your choice, preferably spaghetti or linguine

Cold-pressed olive oil, for drizzling

200 g / 7 oz soft goat's cheese

Fresh flat-leaf parsley, to garnish

ONE-POT CLEANSING KICHADI

3 medium yellow onions

2 medium carrots

1 large tomato

110 g / 3¾ oz mung beans or brown lentils, soaked if possible

1 tbsp coconut oil or ghee

1½ tsp cumin seeds

1½ tsp mustard seeds

1½ tsp coriander seeds

½ tsp ground turmeric

1 cinnamon stick

1 tsp fine sea salt

2 tbsp peeled, very finely chopped fresh ginger

150 g / 5½ oz green beans, fresh or frozen

200 g / 7 oz brown rice, soaked if possible

1 litre / 1¾ pints water

150 g / 5½ oz green peas, fresh or frozen

2 handfuls of finely chopped fresh coriander, to serve

ROLLOVER Turn any leftovers of this stew into a savoury breakfast the next day with a poached egg and some stir-fried greens.

Kichadi, sometimes called and spelled khichdi, kitchari, kitcheree or khichri, is the famous one-pot Indian dish that combines rice and lentils or quick-cooking pulses such as mung beans. It's best known in Ayurvedic tradition as a complete protein meal; it's also very easy to digest and a cinch to make!

Because of its simplicity and ease, many people find that doing a detox on kichadi is very pleasant and far less of an undertaking than a juice fast, for example. Eating this dish exclusively for three to five days is said to purify the digestive organs while cleansing the body of toxins. I like to do this in the winter months when the weather is cold and I need some grounding, warm food and juicing seems out of the question.

Soaking the rice and lentils together overnight is rather important for improving the digestive qualities of kichadi, but if you are pressed for time, you can skip this step.

SERVES 6–8 ———————————————————

1 Prepare the vegetables: dice the onions, and chop the carrots and tomato. Set aside in separate bowls. Drain and rinse the mung beans.

2 In a large stockpot or pan, melt the coconut oil over a medium heat. Add the cumin and mustard seeds and fry just until the mustard seeds start to pop. Stir in the coriander, turmeric, cinnamon stick and salt, then add the ginger and tomato. Cook for about 2 minutes until fragrant.

3 Add the onions, carrots, green beans, rice, mung beans, peas and the water. Bring to the boil, reduce the heat to low and simmer, covered, for about 45 minutes until the rice and beans are soft. Add more water if the pot becomes dry while cooking or to achieve a more stew-like consistency.

4 Season with salt and serve with the coriander.

SWEET POTATO, CAULIFLOWER AND COCONUT CASSEROLE

Perhaps they're a tad retro, but casseroles are undeniably comforting. This one features a unique combination of sweet potatoes, cauliflower and coconut milk steeped in warming spices, and a satisfying crunchy nut topping. To change things a little, simply try a different spice blend, or use dried herbs instead, such as rosemary and thyme. Serve this with a fresh green salad on the side for extra nutrients and to complement the warming, grounding nature of the casserole.

SERVES 6

1 Preheat the oven to 200°C / 400°F / Gas mark 6. In a small bowl, whisk together the coconut milk, tamari, spices and a few pinches of salt.

2 Make the topping: in a food processor, pulse the almonds, sunflower seeds, oats, ½ teaspoon of salt and the pepper until crumbly. Add the coconut oil and 2 tablespoons of the coconut milk mixture and pulse until it holds together when pressed.

3 Cut the sweet potato and cauliflower into 8 mm / ⅓ in thick slices. Alternating between sweet potato and cauliflower, layer the slices horizontally in a 23 x 33 cm / 9 x 13 in baking tin, seasoning with more salt as you go. Stuff leftover pieces of cauliflower in the spaces between the vegetables.

4 Pour the coconut milk mixture over the vegetables. Spread the almond topping over the top, squeezing a few bits of it together here and there so that you create some chunks. Cover the dish with foil, making sure to seal the sides.

5 Bake for 30–35 minutes until the vegetables are tender but not mushy, then remove the foil and continue baking for a further 10 minutes until the topping browns. Garnish with fresh parsley, if liked. Serve hot.

1 400 ml / 14 fl oz can full-fat coconut milk

1 tbsp gluten-free tamari or soy sauce

¼ tsp each ground cloves, cardamom and freshly grated nutmeg

½ tsp fine sea salt, plus extra as needed

75 g / 2¾ oz raw, unsalted almonds

80 g / 3 oz raw, unsalted, shelled sunflower seeds

100 g / 3½ oz gluten-free rolled oats

1 tsp freshly ground black pepper

2 tbsp coconut oil

1 large / 500 g (1 lb 2 oz) sweet potato, unpeeled

1 head of cauliflower

Handful of fresh flat-leaf parsley or fresh coriander leaves, to garnish (optional)

SAVOURY LEEK AND MUSHROOM GALETTE

DOUGH

300 g / 10½ oz wholegrain wheat flour

50 g / 1¾ oz rolled oats

¼ tsp fine sea salt

115 ml / 4 fl oz coconut oil, cold

185 ml / 6½ fl oz iced water

FILLING

1 tbsp ghee or coconut oil

350 g / 12 oz leeks, chopped, white and light-green parts only

1 tsp fine sea salt

3 garlic cloves, very finely chopped

1 tbsp dried thyme

1 tsp freshly ground black pepper

3 large portobello mushrooms, sliced

50 g / 1¾ oz baby spinach leaves

1 tbsp freshly squeezed lemon juice

100 g / 3½ oz feta cheese (preferably goat's or sheep's)

Fresh flat-leaf parsley leaves, to garnish (optional)

If pastry intimidates you, behold the galette. Easy to make and hard to mess up, this foolproof tart can be mastered by anyone. Although one would normally think of this as a sweet dessert, this recipe is deliciously savoury and makes a main dish far more impressive than the effort that went into it. The filling is a richly seasoned combination of creamy leeks and mushrooms with an honest dose of spinach that cleverly melts into the mix and doesn't overwhelm. The crust is hearty and satisfying, with crunchy edges that complement the tender filling. If you would prefer a vegan dish, simply leave out the feta cheese and use coconut oil instead of ghee.

SERVES 4–6

1 Prepare the dough: place the flour, oats and salt in a large bowl and stir to combine. Cut the cold coconut oil into pieces and add it to the bowl. Use a pastry cutter or a couple of forks to cut the oil into the flour until the mixture has a pea-like consistency. Drizzle in about 5 tablespoons of the iced water and continue to mix the ingredients until a small amount of it holds together when squeezed. You may need to add more water, up to 185 ml / 6½ fl oz. Do not overwork the dough or add too much water or the pastry will be tough and chewy.

2 Gather the dough into a rough ball in the bowl, then transfer it to a piece of clingfilm. Wrap the dough ball in the clingfilm and flatten it into a rough disc. Chill the dough in the fridge for at least an hour and up to 2 days.

(recipe continues)

3 Make the filling: in a large frying pan, melt the ghee over a medium-high heat. Add the leeks and salt, stir to coat and cook for about 10 minutes until the leeks soften and are slightly caramelized. Add the garlic, thyme, pepper and mushrooms, stir to coat and cook for 5–7 minutes until the mushrooms have softened. Remove from the heat, add the spinach and lemon juice and stir until the spinach has wilted.

4 Preheat the oven to 200°C / 400°F / Gas mark 6.

5 Remove the dough from the clingfilm. Place it between 2 large pieces of baking paper, and roll it out into a 36 cm / 14 in round. Peel off the top piece of baking paper.

6 Add the filling to the dough disc and spread it evenly, leaving 5 cm / 2 in space around the edges. Crumble the feta over the top and fold about 4 cm / 1½ in of the crust's edge over onto the filling all around. Slide the baking paper with the galette onto a rimmed baking sheet and bake for 35–40 minutes until the pastry is golden and cooked through.

7 Slice the galette into wedges, sprinkle with parsley, if liked, and enjoy hot or at room temperature.

ROLLOVER **Double the dough recipe, freeze half and make a galette next season using totally different produce. This would be lovely with a filling of mixed roasted veggies, such as pumpkin, beetroot and sweet potatoes.**

GRILLED AUBERGINE AND MUSHROOMS

with Saucy Almond Butter Noodles

There is something undeniably satisfying about a big noodle bowl smothered in delicious sauce and piled high with colourful veggies. It's the kind of thing I'm in the mood for any time of year. I really like grilling the aubergines and mushrooms, but you can also roast them in the oven if you don't feel like firing up the barbecue, or if you don't have a stovetop grill pan. If you're feeling ambitious, make a batch of the Ginger-pickled Carrots (page 87) to serve here; their tender crunch and bright acidity really round out the dish.

SERVES 4

2 medium aubergines

4 portobello mushrooms, stems removed

35 g / 1¼ oz raw, unsalted sesame seeds

250 g / 9 oz dried rice noodles (preferably brown rice noodles)

Almond Butter Sauce (recipe follows)

Ginger-pickled Carrots (optional, but delicious; page 87)

10 g / ¼ oz chopped fresh coriander

1 Preheat your grill to high. Slice the aubergines into 1.3 cm / ½ in rounds and the mushrooms into 0.5 cm / ¼ in slices. Place the vegetables on the grill and cook for about 5 minutes until softened and marked on the underside. Flip and grill on the other side for a further 3–4 minutes until the vegetables are softened and charred.

2 Preheat a small dry frying pan over a medium heat. When hot, toast the sesame seeds, stirring frequently, for 2–3 minutes until fragrant. Immediately remove the pan from the heat and set it aside.

3 Fill a medium saucepan with water and bring to the boil. Add the rice noodles and cook until tender, according to the packet instructions. Drain and set aside.

4 To serve, place about a quarter of the noodles on each plate. Top with grilled veggies and pour the Almond Butter Sauce over the top. Garnish with Ginger-pickled Carrots, if liked, coriander and sesame seeds.

(recipe continues)

ALMOND BUTTER SAUCE

MAKES ABOUT 250 ML / 8 FL OZ

In a blender, combine the almond butter, garlic, tamari, maple syrup, ginger, lime juice, chilli and water, and blend until smooth and creamy. Taste and season with salt, if necessary.

ROLLOVER Make an extra batch of Almond Butter Sauce and use it for the Run Wild Summer Rolls (page 101).

125 g / 4½ oz almond butter

2 small garlic cloves

2 tbsp gluten-free tamari or soy sauce

1 tbsp pure maple syrup

½ tsp peeled, very finely chopped fresh ginger

6 tbsp freshly squeezed lime juice (from approximately 2 limes)

1 small red chilli, stem and seeds removed (Serrano is a good choice)

125 ml / 4 fl oz water

Sea salt

BUTTER BEAN GINGER STEW

1 tbsp coconut oil or ghee

250 g / 9 oz leeks, chopped, white and light-green parts only (onions will also work)

Fine sea salt

2 tsp ground turmeric

Pinch of cayenne pepper

3 bay leaves

5 garlic cloves, sliced

1½ tsp peeled, very finely chopped fresh ginger

1 400 g / 14 oz can whole peeled tomatoes

4 medium carrots, scrubbed

625 ml / 22 fl oz vegetable stock

3 lemon slices

1½ tsp pure maple syrup

225 g / 8 oz (1 240 g / 8½ oz can) cooked butter beans (any white bean will work), drained and rinsed

50 g / 1¾ oz baby spinach leaves

Cold-pressed olive oil, to serve

Freshly ground black pepper, to serve

Butter beans undoubtedly live up to their name: deliciously creamy and melt-in-your-mouth tender. Instead of blending them up to make a dip (which would be a shame!), I enjoy them in soups, stews and salads, where I can really get the most out of their impressive size and unique texture. In this simple, nourishing recipe, butter beans are combined with stewed tomatoes and carrots, warming ginger, turmeric and cayenne, with a touch of lemon for brightness. Instead of cooking the spinach, you'll add it just before serving so that it just wilts, retaining many of its delicate nutrients. Make a double batch of this and freeze leftovers for a heat-and-eat meal when you're tempted to order a takeaway!

SERVES 3–4

1 In a large stockpot or pan, melt the coconut oil over a medium heat. Add the leeks and a couple of pinches of salt, the turmeric, cayenne and bay leaves. Cook for about 5 minutes until the leeks have softened, then add the garlic and ginger. If the pot becomes dry, add a little liquid from the canned tomatoes.

2 Slice the carrots into quarters lengthways and then in half across their width so that you end up with batons. Add the carrots, tomatoes and their liquid, vegetable stock, lemon slices and maple syrup to the pot. Bring to the boil, reduce the heat to low and simmer for 15–20 minutes until the carrots are tender but not mushy.

3 Add the cooked butter beans to the pot, stir and let them heat through, 3–4 minutes. Remove from the heat and fold in the spinach – it will wilt from the residual heat. Serve with a drizzle of olive oil and a few grinds of black pepper.

ROLLOVER Make this stew even more substantial by serving it on top of Copycat Couscous with Clementines (page 175).

SPROUTED LENTIL CHILLI

1 tbsp coconut oil or ghee

2 medium yellow onions, diced

1 medium leek, white and light-green parts only, diced

1 tsp fine sea salt, plus extra as needed

5 garlic cloves, very finely chopped

1½ tsp ground cumin

1½ tsp ground coriander

1 tsp ground cinnamon

½ tsp ground chipotle

1 small red chilli (stem and seeds removed), sliced (Serrano is a good choice)

50 g / 1¾ oz sun-dried tomatoes (about 8), roughly chopped

1 medium red pepper (stem, seeds and ribs removed), diced

500 g / 1 lb 2 oz sweet potatoes and/or carrots, diced

625 ml / 22 fl oz vegetable stock

1 400 g / 14 oz can chopped tomatoes

170 g / 6 oz lentil sprouts (see Basic Sprouts, page 23)

Here's a fun take on classic chilli – using sprouted lentils instead of beans. The result is a much lighter chilli that leaves you feeling satisfied but not stuffed. The sprouted lentils aid digestion and give you a huge boost of protein, fibre and minerals. Remember that sprouts take about three days to grow, so make sure you start this meal well in advance! If you've never made your own sprouts before, check out the simple instructions on page 23. If you're pressed for time, you can also purchase beansprouts from the supermarket or health food store. The topping for the chilli is also delicious on toast or crackers, in a wrap or simply folded through simple greens for an instant salad.

SERVES 4

1 In a large stockpot or pan, melt the coconut oil over a medium heat. Add the onions, leek and salt, and stir to coat. Cook for 10 minutes until the onions soften and begin to slightly caramelize. Add the garlic and spices and cook for about 2 minutes until fragrant.

2 Add the chilli, sun-dried tomatoes, red pepper and sweet potatoes and cook for a further 5 minutes, adding a little stock to the pot if it becomes dry.

3 Add the canned tomatoes with their juices, along with the vegetable stock. Bring to the boil, reduce the heat to low and cook for 15–20 minutes until the sweet potatoes are tender. Remove from the heat and keep warm.

4 Meanwhile, make the topping: in a small bowl, combine the 85 g / 3 oz lentil sprouts, lime juice, salt, olive oil, avocado and coriander.

5 Stir the 170 g / 6 oz sprouted lentils into the chilli. Season with salt. Serve in bowls with a scoop of the topping and a drizzle of olive oil.

TOPPING

85 g / 3 oz lentil sprouts
(see Basic Sprouts, page 23)

Juice of ½ lime

Pinch of fine sea salt

1 tbsp cold-pressed olive oil,
plus extra to serve

1 ripe avocado, cubed

Small handful of fresh
coriander, roughly chopped

POLENTA

with Beetroot Ribbons and Rocket Pesto

If you're looking to serve something impressive and restaurant-worthy to guests, this dish is sure to fit the bill. Creamy polenta, rich rocket pesto and sweet, earthy beetroot combine to create a harmonious, not to mention beautiful, meal. By simply slicing the roasted beetroot into thin ribbons and curling them around each other, you'll end up with such a spectacular presentation that it will look like you've been to culinary school.

There are three elements to this dish, but both the roasted beetroot and the pesto can be made up to three days ahead of time, so all you have to do before serving is cook the polenta, making this very doable on a weeknight when you want to put something special on the table.

SERVES 4 ——————————————————————————

1 Preheat the oven to 200°C / 400°F / Gas mark 6. Wrap the beetroot in foil and place it on a rimmed baking sheet. Roast for about 45 minutes. The beetroot is ready when you can easily insert a sharp knife into the centre. Remove it from the oven, peel back the foil a little and leave it to cool. When the beetroot is cool, slip the skins off.

2 While the beetroot is roasting, make the polenta. In a large saucepan, heat the vegetable stock and a good pinch of salt until it begins to simmer. Slowly pour in the polenta in a steady stream, whisking all the while to prevent clumping. Whisk constantly for a couple of minutes, then reduce the heat to low and cover the saucepan. Stir every 5 minutes or so until the polenta is creamy without any grit to it, 30–45 minutes total. If the polenta becomes too thick, whisk in a little hot water or more vegetable stock.

3 While the polenta is cooking, make the pesto: lower the oven temperature to 180°C / 350°F / Gas mark 4.

2 medium red beetroot

1–1.5 litres / 1¾–2½ pints vegetable stock or salted water

Fine sea salt

160 g / 5¾ oz polenta (cornmeal)

ROCKET PESTO

50 g / 1¾ oz raw, unsalted walnuts

1 small garlic clove

50 g / 1¾ oz rocket

30 g / 1 oz Pecorino Romano, freshly grated (about 6 tbsp; Parmesan will also work)

1 tbsp freshly squeezed lemon juice

2 tbsp cold-pressed olive oil

Fine sea salt

100 g / 3½ oz feta (preferably sheep's or goat's)

1 tbsp cold-pressed olive oil, for drizzling

Sea salt flakes and freshly ground black pepper, to serve

(recipe continues)

4 Place the walnuts on a rimmed baking sheet and toast them in the oven for 7–10 minutes, watching them so they do not burn. Remove from the oven and leave to cool slightly.

5 In a food processor, pulse the garlic until very finely chopped. Add the walnuts and pulse to very finely chop. Add the rocket, Pecorino, lemon juice and olive oil, and pulse until uniform. Season with salt. (The pesto will keep in an airtight container in the fridge for up to 3 days.)

6 Place the peeled beetroot on a chopping board and slice off the ends. Using a vegetable peeler, slice the beetroot into strips. Set aside.

7 To assemble, spoon about a quarter of the polenta onto each plate and top each with the desired amount of pesto. Roll up the beetroot ribbons and sink them down into the pesto and polenta. Curl more beetroot pieces in and around the rolls until most of the polenta is covered. Crumble the feta over the top, drizzle with olive oil and sprinkle with salt and pepper.

ROLLOVER Spread leftover pesto on toasted wholegrain bread and top with a poached egg.

CEREMONIAL STUFFED PUMPKIN

with Bulgur Wheat, Feta and Figs

This is celebration food: a dish to gather friends and family and one that marks an occasion. Serve this stuffed pumpkin at an autumn harvest or throughout the holiday season for an impressive centrepiece that will tell everyone at your table how much you care. There is a bit of everything going on in this meal, which is why it is so darn delicious. Sweet roasted pumpkin, chewy bulgur, lemony kale, salty feta, crispy pumpkin seeds, chewy dried figs and sharp onion – a deluge of tastes and textures! If you cannot find bulgur wheat, use brown rice or wholewheat couscous instead. I like to massage the kale for a couple of minutes before adding the remaining ingredients. This step is optional, but it's a simple, cool trick that creates a much sweeter and tenderer green!

SERVES 4 —————————————————————————

175 g / 6 oz bulgur wheat

500 ml / 18 fl oz water

½ tsp fine sea salt, plus extra as needed

1 garlic clove, very finely chopped

1 tbsp cold-pressed olive oil, plus extra for massaging the kale

1 tbsp freshly squeezed lemon juice

1 small (1.5 kg / 3 lb 5 oz) pumpkin or winter squash, such as Hokkaido or acorn

Coconut oil or ghee, for rubbing the pumpkin

1 Rinse the bulgur wheat well and place it in a pot with the water and the salt. Bring to the boil, reduce the heat to low and cook, covered, for 25–35 minutes until the grains are tender but still a little al dente. Immediately stir in the garlic, olive oil and lemon juice while the bulgur wheat is still hot, and season with more sea salt, if liked. Remove from heat and re-cover so the grains stay warm.

2 While the bulgur wheat is cooking, roast the pumpkin. Preheat the oven to 200°C / 400°F / Gas mark 6. Wash the outside of the pumpkin thoroughly – you will be eating the skin as well as the flesh. Slice around the stem, including a good amount of flesh; this will be your 'lid'. Scoop out the seeds. Rub the inside, outside and the lid with a little coconut oil or ghee. Place the pumpkin with its lid on a rimmed baking sheet and roast for 25–30 minutes. The pumpkin is cooked when a knife can be easily inserted into the flesh.

(recipe continues)

FILLING

120 g / 4¼ oz kale, shredded

1 tbsp cold-pressed olive oil

1 tbsp freshly squeezed lemon juice

½ tsp fine sea salt

30 g / 1 oz raw, unsalted pumpkin seeds

225 g / 8 oz (1 240 g / 8½ oz can) cooked chickpeas, drained and rinsed

4 large dried figs (75 g / 2¾ oz), roughly chopped

1 small red onion or 2 shallots, thinly sliced

A few pinches of crushed chilli flakes (optional)

80 g / 3 oz crumbled feta (preferably goat's or sheep's)

3 Meanwhile, prepare the filling: in a large bowl, combine the kale, the olive oil, lemon juice and salt. Using your hands, rub and squeeze the kale together as if you are giving it a massage, until the kale leaves are dark green and tender, about 2 minutes.

4 In a dry frying pan over a medium heat, toast the pumpkin seeds for 3–5 minutes until fragrant.

5 In a very large bowl, combine the bulgur wheat, chickpeas, kale, figs, onion, pumpkin seeds, chilli flakes, if using, and feta. Toss to coat and season with salt.

6 To serve, stuff as much of the filling as you can into the pumpkin. Place the lid on the pumpkin, or let the filling spill out onto the platter and serve the lid on the side. Cut the pumpkin into wedges and serve with the filling on top.

ROLLOVER This filling recipe makes enough for 2 stuffed pumpkins or 1 pumpkin with plenty left over; use it to replace the Sunflower Meta Feta in the Aubergine Cannelloni with Sunflower Feta and Toasted Garlic Tomato Sauce (page 114).

WILD RICE, ROASTED CARROT AND POMEGRANATE BOLD BOWL

This is, quite simply, a bold bowl of yumminess! The nutty flavour from the wild rice pairs so well with the sweetness of carrots and tangy burst of pomegranate seeds. A drizzle of Toasted Walnut Sauce takes it over the top. Serve this bright delight during the holiday season, when pomegranates are ripe and juicy. It can easily be the centrepiece of the meal or a tasty side dish to accompany a feast of other cold-weather favourites.

SERVES 4 ————————————————————————

1 Rinse the wild rice, then place it in a small saucepan with ½ teaspoon of salt. Cover with plenty of water and bring to the boil. Reduce the heat to low and cook, covered, for 45–60 minutes until the rice is tender and chewy.

2 While the rice is cooking, roast the carrots. Preheat the oven to 200°C / 400°F / Gas mark 6. Slice the carrots lengthways into halves or quarters, depending on their size, and place them on a rimmed baking sheet with the coconut oil. Place the baking sheet in the oven to melt the coconut oil, remove it from the oven and toss the carrots to coat, then sprinkle with 2 pinches of sea salt. Return the carrots to the oven and roast for 15–20 minutes until they are blistered and tender.

3 Remove the pomegranate seeds from the fruit and roughly chop the parsley. In a large bowl, toss the cooked wild rice with about half of the Toasted Walnut Sauce and the carrots, chickpeas, pomegranate seeds and parsley. Serve warm or at room temperature with the extra dressing on the side.

ROLLOVER Roast twice as many carrots to make Smoky Roasted Carrot Hummus (page 188).

120 g / 4¼ oz wild rice, soaked overnight if possible

½ tsp fine sea salt, plus extra as needed

225 g / 8 oz carrots, scrubbed

2 tsp coconut oil or ghee

1 pomegranate

30 g / 1 oz fresh flat-leaf parsley leaves

Toasted Walnut Sauce (page 84)

225 g / 8 oz (1 240 g / 8½ oz can) cooked chickpeas, drained and rinsed

CAULIFLOWER STEAKS

with Chermoula and Eggs

2 heads of cauliflower

1 tbsp coconut oil or ghee

Fine sea salt

CHERMOULA

1 garlic clove

2 pinches of fine sea salt

½ tsp freshly ground black pepper

¼ tsp smoked hot paprika (ground chipotle would also work)

½ tsp crushed chilli flakes

1 tsp ground cumin

½ tsp ground coriander

4 tbsp cold-pressed olive oil

4 tbsp freshly squeezed lemon juice

60 g / 2¼ oz fresh flat-leaf parsley leaves, plus extra to garnish

60 g / 2¼ oz fresh coriander leaves, plus extra to garnish

4–8 large eggs
(1–2 eggs per person)

Chermoula is a spicy flavour bomb of a sauce from North Africa, typically used to marinate meat and fish, but it is wildly delicious with veggies too. Here I've paired it with big slabs of roasted cauliflower and a poached egg, making a substantial and truly satisfying meal. If you can multitask, this dish comes together easily in thirty minutes.

SERVES 4 ———————————————————

1 Preheat the oven to 200°C / 400°F / Gas mark 6. Cut the cauliflower from top to bottom into 1.3 cm / ½ in thick slices. Save any florets or small pieces for another dish. Rub the cauliflower with the coconut oil and season with salt. Place it on a large rimmed baking sheet and roast for 20–30 minutes until golden and tender but not mushy.

2 While the cauliflower is roasting, make the chermoula: in a food processor, pulse the garlic until very finely chopped. Add the salt, pepper, spices, oil and lemon juice and pulse to combine. Roughly chop the herbs, add them and pulse until the desired consistency is reached – it's delicious smooth or left a little chunky. (This step can be done ahead of time; leftovers keep in an airtight container in the fridge for up to 4 days.)

3 Poach the eggs: bring a shallow pot of water to a simmer over a low heat. Gently stir the water to create a whirlpool. Crack 1 egg into a small dish, then carefully transfer the egg to the centre of the whirlpool. Poach the egg for 3–4 minutes. Remove the egg from the water with a slotted spoon and place it on a clean kitchen towel to absorb any water. Repeat with the remaining eggs.

4 To serve, place a generous dollop of chermoula (about 4 tablespoons, or more as desired) on each plate, followed by 2 cauliflower steaks. Season the cauliflower with salt, add 1 or 2 poached eggs and top with a sprinkling of fresh herbs. Enjoy immediately.

ROLLOVER Fold any extra chermoula into warm or cold cooked grains, or use it like a pesto over pasta. I also really love it on toast with an egg for breakfast – a great way to start your day with a download of nourishing herbs!

simple sides and
SMALL PLATES

—

PREVIOUS PAGE, from left to right: Beetroot and Butter Beans with Lemon and Mint, page 153 / Beetroot with Avocado, Sesame and Ginger, page 154 / Balsamic Beetroot with Hazelnuts, Parsley and Pomegranate, page 155

ROASTED BEETROOT, 3 WAYS

Roasting beetroot brings out the incredible depth and sweetness in these roots, giving them a rich, caramelized taste. These three salads show the versatility of roasted beetroot and its ability to become a blank canvas for so many international flavours. I like to cook a large amount of beetroot at the beginning of the week to use in a variety of dishes, or I keep it as the star of the show, as in the tantalizing recipes below. Roasted beetroot will keep in an airtight container in the fridge for up to four days.

BEETROOT AND BUTTER BEANS
with Lemon and Mint

SERVES 3–4

1 Preheat the oven to 200°C / 400°F / Gas mark 6. Wrap each beetroot individually in foil and place them on a rimmed baking sheet. Roast for 30–60 minutes, depending on the size of the beetroot. The beetroot is ready when you can insert a sharp knife into the centre without too much resistance – it should be tender, not mushy. When it is cool enough to handle, peel off and discard the skins, cut the beetroot into bite-sized chunks and place it in a bowl.

2 Preheat a dry frying pan over a medium heat. When hot, toast the pumpkin seeds, tossing frequently, for 3–5 minutes until fragrant. Remove the pan from the heat and set aside.

3 In a small bowl, whisk together the olive oil, lemon zest and juice, maple syrup and a pinch of salt. Pour the dressing over the beetroot, then fold in the mint, butter beans and pumpkin seeds. Season with salt.

750 g / 1 lb 10 oz beetroot

25 g / 1 oz raw, unsalted pumpkin seeds

2 tbsp cold-pressed olive oil

Zest of 1 lemon

2 tbsp freshly squeezed lemon juice

½ tsp pure maple syrup

Fine sea salt

10 g / ¼ oz chopped fresh mint

225 g / 8 oz (1 240 g / 8½ oz can) cooked butter beans, drained and rinsed

BEETROOT
with Avocado, Sesame and Ginger

(V) (GF) (GrF)

750 g / 1 lb 10 oz beetroot

2 tbsp raw, unsalted sesame seeds

2 tsp peeled, very finely chopped fresh ginger

2 tbsp freshly squeezed lime juice

2 tbsp cold-pressed olive oil

2 ripe avocados

2 generous pinches of sea salt flakes

SERVES 3–4 ─────────────

1 Preheat the oven to 200°C / 400°F / Gas mark 6. Wrap each beetroot individually in foil and place them on a rimmed baking sheet. Roast for 30–60 minutes, depending on the size of the beetroot. The beetroot is ready when you can insert a sharp knife into the centre without too much resistance – it should be tender, not mushy. Remove the beetroot from the oven, peel back the foil a little and leave to cool. When it is cool enough to handle, peel off and discard the skins, cut the beetroot into bite-sized chunks and place it in a bowl.

2 Preheat a dry frying pan over a medium heat. When hot, toast the sesame seeds, stirring frequently, for 2–3 minutes until fragrant and beginning to pop. Remove the pan from the heat and set aside.

3 In a small bowl, whisk together the very finely chopped ginger, lime juice and olive oil. Pour this dressing over the beetroot, add half of the sesame seeds and fold to combine.

4 To serve, slice the avocados into thin sections and fan them out on a large platter. Spoon the beetroot over the top, sprinkle with the remaining sesame seeds and season with the salt. Serve immediately.

BALSAMIC BEETROOT

with Hazelnuts, Parsley and Pomegranate

V   GF   GrF

SERVES 3–4 ———————————————

1 Preheat the oven to 200°C / 400°F / Gas mark 6. Wrap each beetroot individually in foil and place them on a rimmed baking sheet. Roast for 30–60 minutes, depending on the size of the beetroot. The beetroot is ready when you can insert a sharp knife into the centre without too much resistance – it should be tender, not mushy. Remove the beetroot from the oven, peel back the foil a little and leave to cool. When it is cool enough to handle, peel off and discard the skins, cut the beetroot into bite-sized chunks and place it in a bowl.

2 While the beetroot is roasting, place the hazelnuts on another rimmed baking sheet and place them in the oven. Roast for 10–15 minutes until they are toasted and fragrant. Remove from the oven, leave to cool slightly, then rub off their skins and roughly chop the hazelnuts.

3 In a small bowl, whisk together the olive oil, balsamic, Dijon, salt and pepper. Pour this dressing over the beetroot, toss to coat, then add the parsley, hazelnuts and pomegranate seeds. Fold to combine.

SIDES ME UP! All of these salads would be delicious in a wrap or pitta bread, or on top of cooked grains such as brown rice or quinoa, for a complete meal.

ROLLOVER Roast extra beetroot to make the Polenta with Beetroot Ribbons and Rocket Pesto (page 141).

750 g / 1 lb 10 oz beetroot

55 g / 2 oz raw, unsalted hazelnuts

1½ tsp cold-pressed olive oil

1½ tsp balsamic vinegar

1½ tsp Dijon mustard

2 pinches of fine sea salt

Freshly ground black pepper

15 g / ½ oz chopped fresh flat-leaf parsley

90 g / 3¼ oz pomegranate seeds (from about 1 pomegranate)

ROASTED RADISHES AND AVOCADO
with Sesame Salt

15–20 radishes

1 tbsp coconut oil, melted

1 large ripe avocado

Juice of 1 lemon

Handful of fresh chives, very finely chopped

Sesame Salt, to serve (recipe follows)

Although enjoying radishes raw is definitely the norm, I'm all about cooking them for a seriously surprising change of pace. I can't believe just how different and tasty these rose-hued roots become with a little heat! Here I've roasted them, dialling down their distinctive bite; this allows their sweetness to shine through. Paired with creamy avocado, bright lemon and Sesame Salt, this is a simple little side dish that would be a delicious way to start a meal.

SIDES ME UP! To make this a meal, serve this salad over cooked brown rice, topped with crunchy sprouts.

SERVES 3–4

1 Preheat the oven to 200°C / 400°F / Gas mark 6. Slice the radishes in half, place them on a rimmed baking sheet and toss with the coconut oil. Roast for about 20 minutes until the radishes are tender and blistered in places. Remove them from the oven and leave to cool slightly.

2 Stone and peel the avocado, and then cut the flesh into cubes, about half the size of the radishes. Evenly divide the avocado cubes among individual plates, repeat with the radishes and then pour half the lemon juice over the vegetables, adding more if liked. Sprinkle the chives and Sesame Salt over the top.

SESAME SALT
MAKES APPROXIMATELY 75 G / 2¾ OZ

75 g / 2¾ oz raw, unsalted sesame seeds

1½ tsp fine sea salt

In a large dry frying pan, toast the sesame seeds over a medium heat, stirring occasionally, for 2–3 minutes until fragrant, being careful not to burn them. Remove from the heat and transfer the seeds to a food processor or mortar. Add the salt and process until about half the seeds are broken. The mixture will keep in an airtight jar at room temperature for up to 2 months.

KALE, MUSHROOMS AND WALNUTS

with Pecorino

35 g / 1¼ oz raw, unsalted walnuts

1 small onion

2 garlic cloves

250 g / 9 oz chestnut mushrooms

1½ tsp coconut oil or ghee

Fine sea salt

½ tsp dried thyme

60 g / 2¼ oz kale, chopped

1 tbsp balsamic vinegar

Freshly ground black pepper

1 tbsp cold-pressed olive oil (optional)

Freshly grated Pecorino Romano or Parmesan, to serve

ROLLOVER Caramelize extra onions for the Portobello Pizzas (page 119).

This little plate is like a walk in the autumn forest: deep, dark and earthy. Grounding mushrooms and greens get a lift from sweet-and-sour vinegar notes and a light dusting of salty cheese. The walnuts add a particularly pleasing crunch, but almonds or pecans would be equally tasty.

SERVES 2–3

1 Preheat a dry frying pan over a medium heat. When hot, toast the walnuts for 3–4 minutes until fragrant and just golden. Remove the pan from the heat, let the nuts cool, then roughly chop them.

2 Prepare the vegetables: slice the onion into thin rounds, very finely chop the garlic and quarter the mushrooms.

3 Wipe the frying pan clean of any walnut skins, then melt 1 teaspoon of the coconut oil over a medium-high heat. Add the onion and a pinch of sea salt and stir to coat. Cook, stirring occasionally, for about 15 minutes until the onions soften and are nicely caramelized. Remove the onions from the pan and set them aside.

4 Without cleaning the frying pan, melt the remaining ghee and add the mushrooms. Cook without stirring until the mushrooms brown on one side, at least 5 minutes. (They will seem dry at first, but they will release their water as they cook.) Give them a shake, and cook for a few minutes more without disturbing them. When the mushrooms are soft and juicy, add the thyme and garlic and cook for a further 1 minute. Add the kale and balsamic vinegar and remove from the heat just as the kale wilts and turns bright green, after about 2 minutes. Season with salt and black pepper. Fold in the caramelized onions, toasted walnuts and olive oil.

5 To serve, place a small mound of the mixture on each plate (or add all of it to a serving platter) and grate the cheese over the top. Enjoy warm.

SIDES ME UP! This meal makes an outstanding
breakfast or lunch when topped with a soft-boiled egg.

GRILLED ASPARAGUS
with Lemony Goat's Cheese Cream

Nothing says spring like those early shoots of green asparagus pushing through the thawing earth; they're also the first sign of life in the supermarket after months of winter. Asparagus is delicious both cooked and raw, and here I've lightly grilled the spears before setting them on a luscious bed of lemon-kissed goat's cheese cream. This sauce pairs really well with roasted vegetables or even simple salad leaves.

SERVES 3–4

1 Heat a grill (or stovetop grill pan) to high. Snap off the tough ends of the asparagus where they naturally break. Coat each spear with just a little of the coconut oil.

2 Place the asparagus on the grill and cook for about 5 minutes on one side until it has charred slightly. Turn and cook for a few minutes more, until each piece is tender and nicely grilled.

3 Meanwhile, make the cream: blend the goat's cheese, garlic, lemon zest, olive oil and lemon juice in a blender until completely smooth and creamy, adding 1–3 tablespoons of water to thin the sauce, as liked. Season with salt.

4 To serve, place a pool of sauce on each plate, then arrange the desired number of asparagus spears on top. Drizzle with extra olive oil, if liked, and season liberally with salt.

SIDES ME UP! Place the asparagus over cooked wild rice and lentils, top with toasted pistachios and drizzle with the Lemony Goat's Cheese Cream.

ROLLOVER Make double the Lemony Goat's Cheese Cream to serve with Terrific Tarragon Green Bean Salad (page 68).

ASPARAGUS

450 g / 1 lb (1 bunch) asparagus

1 tsp coconut oil or ghee

Cold-pressed olive oil, to serve (optional)

Fine sea salt

LEMONY GOAT'S CHEESE CREAM

100 g / 3½ oz soft goat's cheese

1 small garlic clove, very finely chopped

Zest of 1 lemon

1½ tsp cold-pressed olive oil

1 tbsp freshly squeezed lemon juice

Fine sea salt

BROWN BUTTER CARROTS

with Pistachios and Dill

If you're still not convinced that simple food can be wildly delicious, give this recipe a try. With just a few humble ingredients, you can have a truly gourmet food experience!

Brown butter is made by cooking butter until the milk solids in it have caramelized, creating a richer, deeper, nutty-flavoured butter. If you cannot find young carrots (look for them in the spring and early summer), use regular large carrots and slice them in half lengthways before roasting. This will also help reduce the cooking time.

SERVES 2

14 young carrots with tops

2 tsp coconut oil or ghee

Fine sea salt

2 tbsp unsalted butter

1 shallot, finely diced

½ tsp Dijon mustard

1½ tsp apple cider vinegar

1 tbsp raw, unsalted pistachios, lightly toasted and chopped

Handful of fresh dill

ROLLOVER Roast twice as many carrots to make the Wild Rice, Roasted Carrot and Pomegranate Bold Bowl (page 147).

1 Preheat the oven to 200°C / 400°F / Gas mark 6. Scrub the carrots well (do not peel them), and trim off all but 2.5 cm / 1 in of the tops. Rub each carrot with a little coconut oil and place them on a rimmed baking sheet. Season with salt and roast for 20–30 minutes until the carrots are tender and blistered.

2 Meanwhile, make the dressing: in a small frying pan, melt the butter over a medium heat. Add the shallot and swirl the pan over the heat until the butter has changed colour from yellow to light brown, 5–7 minutes (the butter can burn quickly, so keep an eye on it). Remove from the heat and pour the butter and shallot mixture into a jar with the mustard, vinegar and a generous pinch of salt. Seal the jar and shake vigorously to blend.

3 Remove the carrots from the oven and place them on a platter. Pour the dressing over them and scatter the pistachios and dill on top. Serve immediately (the dressing will harden if left at room temperature for too long).

SIDES ME UP! Turn this into a complete meal by serving the carrots over cooked green lentils.

MARINATED ROASTED RED PEPPERS

with Chickpeas

4 large red peppers, stems, seeds and ribs removed

1½ tsp coconut oil

3 tbsp cold-pressed olive oil

2 tbsp balsamic vinegar

2 pinches of fine sea salt

¼ tsp freshly ground black pepper

3 tbsp raisins

Handful of fresh, flat-leaf parsley leaves

225 g / 8 oz (1 240 g / 8½ oz can) cooked chickpeas, drained and rinsed

100 g / 3½ oz feta (preferably goat's or sheep's)

ROLLOVER Roast double the amount of red peppers and make Romesco Sauce (page 195).

Something really magical happens when you roast peppers. They turn from rather uptight, rigid (though tasty) fruits to silky smooth, relaxed, languid things that beg to mingle with complementary tastes. In this dish I've combined the sweet peppers with salty feta, bright parsley and tender chickpeas. With a quick soak in a balsamic bath, the flavours of these ingredients become incredibly rich and satisfying for such a small dish.

SERVES 4 ———————————————————————

1 Preheat the oven to 200°C / 400°F / Gas mark 6. Rub the peppers with the coconut oil and place them on a rimmed baking sheet lined with foil. Roast for 35–40 minutes until blistered and blackened in a few places. Remove the peppers from the baking sheet, place them in a bowl and quickly cover it with clingfilm to steam the peppers, which makes the skin very easy to remove. When the peppers are cool enough to handle, remove and discard the skins.

2 While the peppers are roasting, in a medium bowl, whisk together the olive oil, vinegar, salt and pepper. Very finely chop the raisins and chop the parsley.

3 Tear or slice the skinned roasted peppers into large pieces and place them in the bowl with the dressing. Add the chickpeas, toss to coat and leave to marinate for about 15 minutes.

4 Divide the mixture evenly among 4 plates. Sprinkle with the chopped raisins and parsley and crumble the feta over the top. Serve immediately.

SIDES ME UP! Make this a main dish by serving it over cooked quinoa.

CHARRED AUBERGINE BABA GANOUSH

with Pine Nuts

The secret to really good baba ganoush is charring the heck out of the aubergine skin. After years of roasting the aubergines in the oven for this dish, I've finally cracked the code by firing up my gas hob. This process delivers an unmistakable smoky depth and dimension to the dip that you just can't achieve any other way. It's kind of a messy process but worth every piece of ash left behind. Serve this with wholemeal pitta bread or raw sticks of veggies, or tuck it into a lettuce wrap.

MAKES 500 ML / 18 FL OZ

1 Prick the aubergines all over with a fork to help the steam escape when they are roasting. Place the aubergines directly on top of a gas flame (alternatively, you can do this under a grill or on an outdoor barbecue). Cook for 15–20 minutes, using tongs to turn each one frequently so that they char evenly, until the aubergines are completely soft and blackened. Leave them to cool slightly, then cut each one lengthways down the middle and scoop out the flesh into a bowl, discarding any burnt pieces.

2 In a food processor, pulse the garlic until very finely chopped. Add the aubergine flesh, olive oil, salt and lemon juice, and blend until smooth and creamy. Place the baba ganoush in a medium bowl and season with more salt, as liked.

3 Preheat a dry frying pan over a medium heat. When hot, toast the pine nuts for 2–3 minutes until slightly golden. Immediately remove the pan from the heat and sprinkle the nuts over the baba ganoush. Garnish with chopped parsley, if liked, followed by a generous drizzle of olive oil.

3 medium aubergines

1 garlic clove

4 tbsp cold-pressed olive oil, plus extra to serve

¼ tsp fine sea salt, plus extra as needed

2 tsp freshly squeezed lemon juice

2 tbsp raw, unsalted pine nuts

Small handful of fresh flat-leaf parsley leaves, to garnish (optional)

SIDES ME UP! Make this a meal by spreading the creamy baba ganoush onto 2 slices of wholemeal bread or pitta with sliced red peppers, crumbled feta and rocket.

BAKED FETA

with Olives, Peppers and Tomatoes

100 g / 3½ oz cherry tomatoes

½ red pepper, stem, seeds and ribs removed

60 g / 2¼ oz Kalamata olives

2 tsp dried oregano

Pinch each of sea salt and freshly ground black pepper

200 g / 7 oz block feta (preferably goat's or sheep's)

Cold-pressed olive oil, for drizzling

Small handful of fresh flat-leaf parsley leaves, to garnish

Crusty wholemeal bread or pitta, to serve (optional)

Until I discovered this concept, I'd only ever tried feta cold in salads or as part of a meze platter. But *this* is the new hotness. Baked feta is a revelation, especially when smothered with juicy veggies, herbs and olives. It makes the most wonderful starter to a meal, or it could even be served on the side of a large green salad for a weekend lunch. I like drizzling it generously with olive oil and pairing it with crusty bread to soak up all the delectable juices. However simple, this is definitely one of my favourite recipes in the whole book.

SERVES 2–4

1 Preheat the oven to 200°C / 400°F / Gas mark 6.

2 Slice the tomatoes into quarters. Cut the pepper into similarly sized pieces. Stone the olives and roughly chop them. Place everything in a bowl and toss with the oregano, salt and pepper.

3 Place the feta in an ovenproof dish. Top with the vegetable mixture and bake for 20–25 minutes until the vegetables are roasted and the cheese is soft. Just before serving, drizzle with olive oil and sprinkle with parsley. Enjoy the baked cheese straight out of the oven with crusty wholemeal bread or pittas.

SIDES ME UP! Wrap half the block of the feta and the vegetables with a large leaf of romaine lettuce (or a wholemeal wrap), add fresh sprouts and enjoy.

BROCCOLI
with Garlic Ghee and Pine Nuts

We all need to eat more broccoli. Thankfully, this recipe can definitely help in that department. I could sit down and eat an entire bowl of this for dinner – it's *that* tasty. It's also super simple, easy to make and comes together in a matter of minutes, so you have no excuse for not eating more of this protein-rich, phytonutrient all-star.

Remember that ghee is made with unsalted butter, so this dish will need extra seasoning right at the end. I like to hit it with plenty of good sea salt flakes just after pouring the ghee over so that it sticks to the florets. You can use salted butter in a pinch, but cut back on salting the finished dish if you do. To change things up, use cashews instead of the pine nuts.

SERVES 4

1 large head of broccoli

2 tbsp raw, unsalted pine nuts

2 tbsp ghee

2 garlic cloves, very finely chopped

Plenty of sea salt flakes

SIDES ME UP! Make this a main dish by serving the broccoli over wholewheat noodles or pasta.

ROLLOVER Steam double the amount of broccoli for Broccoli Basil Broth with Noodles and Sesame Salt (page 40).

1 Wash the broccoli and cut it into equal-sized florets, including the long stem (just trim off the bottom).

2 In a large pot fitted with a steamer basket, bring a small amount of water to the boil. Add the broccoli, cover and steam for 5–7 minutes until tender-crisp, depending on the size of the florets, being careful not to overcook. Place the broccoli on a serving platter.

3 While the broccoli is cooking, preheat a dry frying pan over a medium heat. When hot, toast the pine nuts for about 3 minutes until slightly golden. Transfer them to a dish and set aside to cool.

4 In the same frying pan, melt the ghee. Add the very finely chopped garlic and fry just until one or two of the pieces starts to turn golden, about 1 minute. Immediately remove from the heat, pour the garlic oil over the broccoli and toss to coat. Scatter the pine nuts on top and sprinkle with salt. Serve warm.

GRILLED SPRING ONIONS

with Lemon-marinated Chickpeas

225 g / 8 oz (1 240 g / 8½ oz can) cooked chickpeas, drained and rinsed

Zest and juice of 1 lemon

Pinch each of fine sea salt and freshly ground black pepper, plus extra as needed

1 tbsp cold-pressed olive oil, plus extra to serve

16 spring onions

2 tsp coconut oil

Sea salt flakes, to serve

Beans are great for marinating because they are wonderful blank canvases for flavour and willingly absorb anything you anoint them with. Here, a simple mixture of lemon, olive oil and black pepper transforms the humble chickpea into a super-tasty base for smoky grilled spring onions – a match made in heaven!

SERVES 2–3

1 In a medium bowl, combine the chickpeas, lemon zest and juice, salt, pepper and olive oil. Stir to coat, cover and leave the chickpeas to marinate at room temperature for at least 15 minutes, or up to 24 hours in the fridge (the longer the better!).

2 Heat a grill (or stovetop grill pan) to high. Wash and slice off the very tops of the spring onions. Lightly rub the onions with the coconut oil and place them on the grill. Cook for 7–10 minutes, turning once or twice, until the onions are tender and slightly charred.

3 Taste the chickpeas and adjust the seasonings, as liked. Place them on a large plate or platter and lay the grilled onions on top. Spoon any extra marinade over the top, drizzle with olive oil and sprinkle with sea salt flakes.

SIDES ME UP! Turn this into a more substantial dish with cooked quinoa and some toasted almonds.

ROLLOVER Marinate extra chickpeas to use in the Rainbow Hummus Bowl (page 74).

COPYCAT COUSCOUS

with Clementines

Celeriac, sometimes referred to as celery root, is one aggressive-looking vegetable, with an appearance that is sure to intimidate just about anyone who isn't familiar with its surprisingly gentle flavour. With a taste similar to celery sticks, but far milder and sweetly nutty, celeriac is incredibly versatile and delicious in many applications. Here I've very finely chopped it in the food processor to make something that resembles couscous, then mixed it with clementines, pumpkin seeds and parsley. This is a simple, delicious and fresh little salad or side dish for the cooler months.

SERVES 3–4 ———————————————————

1 In a food processor, pulse the celeriac with the sea salt and lemon juice until it is very finely chopped. Transfer to a large serving bowl and toss with the olive oil.

2 Preheat a dry frying pan over a medium heat. When hot, toast the pumpkin seeds, tossing frequently, for 4–5 minutes until fragrant. Remove the pan from the heat and set aside.

3 Add the green olives, parsley, clementines, shallot and pumpkin seeds to the bowl with the celeriac. Toss all of the ingredients together and season with salt.

SIDES ME UP! To make this a meal, add some cooked chickpeas or lentils and a drizzle of Minty Tahini Dressing (page 63).

ROLLOVER Double the celeriac couscous and use it instead of bulgur wheat in the Ceremonial Stuffed Pumpkin with Bulgur Wheat, Feta and Figs (page 143).

750 g / 1 lb 10 oz celeriac (about 1 large celeriac), peeled and roughly chopped

½ tsp fine sea salt, plus extra as needed

1 tbsp freshly squeezed lemon juice

2 tbsp cold-pressed olive oil

50 g / 1¾ oz raw, unsalted pumpkin seeds

120 g / 4¼ oz sliced green olives

30 g / 1 oz fresh flat-leaf parsley leaves

2 clementines (tangerines or mandarins will also work), segmented and cut into small chunks

1 shallot, diced

TWINKLE, TWINKLE, JEWELLED RICE

2 small yellow onions or 4 shallots

2 medium carrots

1 orange

Knob of coconut oil or ghee

1½ tsp cumin seeds

1 tsp ground turmeric

4 bay leaves

4 green cardamom pods, crushed

1 cinnamon stick

75 g / 2¾ oz mixed dried fruit (dates, apricots, raisins, cranberries)

400 g / 14 oz brown basmati rice, rinsed (if you can, soak the rice for up to 8 hours)

1 litre / 1¾ pints water

1 tsp fine sea salt, plus extra as needed

70 g / 2½ oz raw, unsalted almonds

12 g / ¼ oz chopped fresh mint leaves

11 g / ¼ oz chopped fresh chives

90 g / 3¼ oz pomegranate seeds (from about 1 pomegranate)

1 lemon, cut into wedges

Cold-pressed olive oil, for drizzling

This golden, glistening, gem-coloured rice dish is inspired by a classic Iranian recipe that features warm, fragrant spices, dried fruits and nuts – and is a true labour of love to make! I've simplified the process by cooking everything together in one pot, and I've made it healthier by replacing white rice with brown. Although the lemon added at the end may seem like an afterthought, it is an essential element of the dish, rounding out the flavours and adding a zesty kick.

SERVES 8

1 Dice the onions and grate the carrots.

2 Using a vegetable peeler or a small sharp knife, peel the rind from the orange, removing as little white pith as possible. Slice the rind into matchstick-sized strips and set aside. Reserve the orange flesh for another use.

3 In a medium pot, melt the coconut oil over a medium heat. Add the cumin seeds and cook for 1 minute until fragrant, then add the turmeric, bay leaves, cardamom pods and the cinnamon stick. Stir to coat with the oil and fry for another minute until fragrant. Next, add the onions, carrots, orange zest and dried fruit. Cook for about 5 minutes until the onion softens.

4 Drain the rice and add it to the pot with the water and salt. Cover the pot, bring the liquid to the boil, then reduce the heat to low and cook for about 45 minutes until the water has evaporated.

5 Roast the almonds: preheat the oven to 150°C / 300°F / Gas mark 2. Spread the almonds on a rimmed baking sheet in a single layer and roast for 20–25 minutes until they are fragrant and slightly darker in colour. (A good way to check is to bite one in half and check the colour in the

centre – it should be golden.) Remove from the oven and leave to cool completely. Roughly chop the almonds.

6 When the rice is finished cooking, remove from the heat. Scoop the rice out onto a large serving platter to cool slightly and to prevent the grains from sticking together. Sprinkle with the herbs, almonds and pomegranate seeds. Fold to incorporate. Taste and adjust the seasoning (you will likely need to add more salt at this stage). Squeeze a few of the lemon wedges over the top.

7 Serve the rice with a drizzle of olive oil and more lemon wedges.

SIDES ME UP! This is delicious with sautéed aubergine or mushrooms, a poached egg and cooked lentils or chickpeas.

CHARRED CABBAGE

with Apple and Toasted Walnut Sauce

Like grilling, charring lends a complexity to underrated veggies like cabbage. Humble, mild foods take on a whole new taste and texture. The trick is not overdoing it – you want to caramelize them, not burn them! I like pairing charred veggies with something rich and creamy, like this Toasted Walnut Sauce. The fresh, diced apple completes this dish with its acidic high note and crunch.

SERVES 3–6

1 small head white cabbage

125 ml / 4 fl oz water

¼ tsp fine sea salt

1½ tsp coconut oil or ghee

1 large apple

1 tsp freshly squeezed lemon juice

Small handful of fresh flat-leaf parsley leaves

Toasted Walnut Sauce, to serve (page 84)

Sea salt flakes, to garnish

1 Remove the outer leaves from the cabbage. Cut the cabbage into 6 wedges, leaving the base stem intact so that the leaves stay together.

2 In a large frying pan, bring the water to a simmer, add the salt and stir to dissolve. Lay the cabbage wedges in the simmering water, cover and steam them for about 5 minutes until tender (the time may vary slightly, depending on the size of your cabbage). Remove the lid, place the cabbage on a plate and discard the water from the pan.

3 Put the frying pan back on the hob and melt the coconut oil over a high heat. When the oil is hot, put the cabbage back in the pan and cook, uncovered and undisturbed, until a good char has developed, about 5 minutes (again, the time may vary slightly, depending on the size of your cabbage). Turn the wedges to brown them on their other sides for a further 5 minutes.

4 While the cabbage is cooking, dice the apple into very small cubes. In a small bowl, toss the apple with the lemon juice. Very finely chop a few parsley leaves and combine them with the apple.

5 To serve, place 1 or 2 cabbage wedges on each plate, add the apple, drizzle the Toasted Walnut Sauce over the top and garnish with sea salt flakes and the remaining parsley.

SIDES ME UP! Make this a main dish by serving it over cooked wild rice.

ROLLOVER Double the Toasted Walnut Sauce to use the extra on the Rocket and Fig Salad with Toasted Walnut Sauce (page 82).

ROASTED BRUSSELS SPROUTS

with Maple Walnuts

MAPLE WALNUTS

75 g / 2¾ oz raw, unsalted walnuts

1 tbsp pure maple syrup

2 pinches of sea salt flakes

BRUSSELS SPROUTS

500 g / 1 lb 2 oz Brussels sprouts

1½ tsp coconut oil or ghee, melted

Maple-mustard Dressing, to serve (page 69)

2 pinches of fine sea salt, to taste

Freshly ground black pepper

30 g / 1 oz pomegranate seeds

ROLLOVER Use the extra pomegranate seeds for the Wild Rice, Roasted Carrot and Pomegranate Bold Bowl (page 147). Make extra Maple Walnuts to top the Brilliant Banana Almond Soft-serve (page 221).

It still amazes me how the simplest things can also be the most complex tasting and delicious. This dish is a prime example of that. Roasted Brussels sprouts combine beautifully with the bright tang of pomegranates and the toasty, caramelized sweetness of Maple Walnuts, which will be your new go-to topping for all manner of roasted veggies and hearty green salads too. There is something so satisfying about chopping them up – shards of condensed syrup crackling under the blade of your knife. You can make them two days in advance to save yourself some time.

SERVES 3–4 —————————————

1 Prepare the walnuts: preheat the oven to 180°C / 350°F / Gas mark 4. Place the walnuts on a baking sheet with the maple syrup and salt. Toss to coat and bake for 7–10 minutes, tossing once after 5 minutes when the walnuts begin to bubble. Remove from the oven and cool completely.

2 Meanwhile, roast the Brussels sprouts: remove any damaged outer leaves from the Brussels sprouts and slice the sprouts in half lengthways. Place them on a baking sheet and toss with the coconut oil to coat. Roast for about 15 minutes until the sprouts are tender but not overcooked.

3 While the sprouts are roasting, roughly chop the cooled walnuts.

4 When the Brussels sprouts are cooked through, remove them from the oven and immediately drizzle them with the Maple-mustard Dressing, toss to coat and season with salt and pepper. Place them in a large bowl or serving platter, then scatter the pomegranate seeds and Maple Walnuts on top. Serve warm.

SIDES ME UP! This dish works really well for dinner when served over cooked lentils.

SO-SIMPLE ROASTED ROOTS
with Dukkah

It seems almost silly to write such an easy recipe, but in truth, roasted veggies form the foundation of so many of my favourite meals. Inexpensive, versatile and practically foolproof to make, they are a great place to start when you want to add more plants to your diet. Try different combinations of vegetables and cut them in creative ways to keep things interesting.

If you're looking for a different party hors d'oeuvre, try serving these roasted veggies with Dukkah, an Egyptian nut and spice blend that is wildly delicious. I like to simply dip the veg in the Dukkah, which gives them a nutty, seasoned coating.

1 kg / 2 lb 4 oz mixed root vegetables, such as sweet potato, carrot, beetroot, parsnip, swede, turnip and onion

1 tbsp coconut oil or ghee

Fine sea salt and freshly ground black pepper

Garnishes of your choice, such as lemon zest, crushed chilli flakes and fresh herbs (parsley, coriander, basil, mint, rosemary, thyme)

Dukkah, to serve (page 26)

SERVES 4

1 Preheat the oven to 180°C / 350°F / Gas mark 4.

2 Peel any vegetables that require peeling (such as beetroot, swede and turnips). Cut the vegetables into similar-sized pieces so that they cook evenly. Place on a rimmed baking sheet with the coconut oil and transfer the baking sheet to the oven.

3 Roast for about 5 minutes until the oil has melted, then remove from the oven and toss to coat. Place them back in the oven and roast for 25–30 minutes until the vegetables are tender but not mushy.

4 Remove from the oven, season the vegetables generously with sea salt and pepper and garnish with fresh herbs, citrus zest and chilli flakes, if liked. Serve with Dukkah. Store leftovers in an airtight container in the fridge for 3–4 days.

ROLLOVER Make extra roasted roots, store them in the fridge and use them to top soups and salads, fold them into cooked whole grains or blend them up with beans for a dip, such as Roast Beetroot and Caper Hummus (page 189).

SIDES ME UP! Roasted veggies can easily turn into a meal simply by adding cooked quinoa or brown rice, black beans or chickpeas, and a poached egg.

SNACKS

SAVOURY

SWEET

PREVIOUS PAGE, from left to right: Smoky Roasted Carrot Hummus, page 188 /
Roast Beetroot and Caper Hummus, page 189 / Superb Herb Hummus, page 188

HUMMUS, 3 WAYS

Need to shake up your hummus game? Try these winners on for size! We'll start with the basic recipe and then add herbs, spices and roasted veggies to the mix for three surprising twists on the classic: Smoky Roasted Carrot Hummus, Superb Herb Hummus and Roast Beetroot and Caper Hummus.

You will have to add salt to suit your taste in these recipes, as salt amounts will vary greatly if you are using canned chickpeas and shop-bought tahini. Start off with a few pinches and work up from there, tasting as you go.

ROLLOVER Use any of these variations in the Rainbow Hummus Bowl (page 74), and all of them are delicious served with the Carrot Cumin Firecrackers (page 207).

BASIC HUMMUS

SERVES 4 ————————————————————————

1 In a food processor, pulse the garlic until it is very finely chopped.

2 Add the tahini, cumin, lemon zest and juice and olive oil, and purée to make a paste.

3 Add the chickpeas, pulse and add up to 4 tablespoons of water to thin as needed until the desired consistency is reached. Season with salt.

4 Store the hummus in an airtight container in the fridge for up to 5 days.

1 garlic clove

4 tbsp tahini

1 tsp ground cumin

Zest of 1 lemon

3 tbsp freshly squeezed lemon juice

2 tbsp cold-pressed olive oil

225 g / 8 oz (1 240 g / 8½ oz can) cooked chickpeas, drained and rinsed

Fine sea salt

SMOKY ROASTED CARROT HUMMUS

3 large carrots

1 tsp coconut oil

Basic Hummus (page 187)

½ tsp smoked hot paprika (ground chipotle would also work)

Pinch of cayenne pepper (optional)

1 tbsp freshly squeezed lemon juice

Fine sea salt

SERVES 4

1 Preheat the oven to 200°C / 400°F / Gas mark 6. Scrub the carrots well and slice them in half lengthways. Rub each carrot with a little of the coconut oil and place them on a rimmed baking sheet.

2 Roast the carrots for 15–20 minutes until they are tender and blistered but not overcooked.

3 Remove the carrots from the oven and place them in a food processor with the hummus, paprika, cayenne and lemon juice. Purée until smooth. Season with salt.

SUPERB HERB HUMMUS

Basic Hummus (page 187)

1½ tsp freshly squeezed lemon juice

1 tbsp cold-pressed olive oil

1½ tsp pure maple syrup

15 g / ½ oz each chopped fresh chives, mint, coriander and flat-leaf parsley

Fine sea salt

SERVES 4

In a food processor, combine the Basic Hummus, lemon juice, olive oil, maple syrup and herbs. Purée until the desired consistency is reached. Season with salt.

ROAST BEETROOT AND CAPER HUMMUS

SERVES 4 —————————————————————————

1 Preheat the oven to 200°C / 400°F / Gas mark 6. Wrap the beetroot individually in foil and place them on a rimmed baking sheet. Roast for about 30 minutes. The beetroot is ready when you can insert a sharp knife into the centre without too much resistance – it should be tender, not mushy. Remove the beetroot from the oven, peel back the foil a little and leave it to cool. When the beetroot is cool enough to handle, peel off and discard the skins, then cut the beetroot into quarters.

2 In a food processor, combine the beetroot, hummus, capers and lemon juice. Purée until the desired consistency is reached. Season with salt.

3 small beetroot

Basic Hummus (page 187)

3 tbsp capers, drained

1 tbsp freshly squeezed lemon juice

Fine sea salt

STONE FRUIT GINGER SALSA
with Baked Corn Chips

When I began working on an organic farm in Northern California, I arrived at the peak of harvest season. But instead of being out in the garden picking fruits and veggies, my job was to process everything that came into the kitchen. At first this seemed like a total blessing, but it became a huge challenge to figure out ways to preserve the abundance of produce so it would last through the winter. After making a few peach pies and tarts for the freezer, I was pretty stumped on what to do with the remaining kilos of fruit. I am not sure how I came up with the idea, but 'salsa' struck me like lightning, and I became the *queen* of peach salsa.

I tried to re-create the recipe I used back on the farm here, with the addition of fresh ginger, which really makes this something special. If you're into preserving, this is a great salsa to make in big batches and preserve. Serve it as a snack with corn chips or alongside grilled vegetables with your main dish.

SERVES 4

1 Wash, stone and dice the stone fruits into very small pieces, then transfer them to a large bowl.

2 Add the chilli, red pepper, shallot, ginger, coriander, lime juice and salt. Taste and adjust the seasoning as needed, and leave to stand at room temperature, to allow the flavours to meld for at least 20 minutes.

3 Serve with Baked Corn Chips (recipe follows) or your favourite corn chips. The salsa does not keep well (unless you preserve it!), so be sure to eat it within 1 day.

ROLLOVER Make a double batch and use it in place of the Radish Coriander Salsa for Quinoa and Black Beans with Radish Coriander Salsa (page 106).

6 medium stone fruits, such as peaches, nectarines or apricots

1 small red chilli (stem and seeds removed), very finely chopped (Serrano is a good choice)

1 small red pepper (stem, seeds and ribs removed), diced

1 tbsp very finely chopped shallot or red onion

1½ tsp peeled, very finely chopped fresh ginger

15 g / ½ oz chopped fresh coriander leaves and tender stems

1½ tsp freshly squeezed lime juice

¼ tsp sea salt flakes

Baked Corn Chips (recipe follows), to serve (optional)

(recipe continues)

8 good-quality corn tortillas

2–3 tbsp coconut oil, melted

Fine sea salt

BAKED CORN CHIPS

SERVES 4–6

1 Preheat the oven to 180°C / 350°F / Gas mark 4.

2 Brush each tortilla round lightly with melted coconut oil on both sides, making sure to cover the edges as well. Sprinkle with salt.

3 Stack the tortillas on top of one another. Cut the stack into eighths. Place the triangular wedges on a rimmed baking sheet, overlapping as little as possible. Bake for 8–12 minutes until the chips are crisp and just turning golden round the edges; they will likely curl up a little on the baking sheet. The chips will continue to crisp up once removed from the oven. When they are completely cool, transfer them to an airtight container. Note that baked chips will become stale much faster than fried ones, so they are best consumed within a couple days.

CHARRED GREEN BEANS

with Romesco Sauce

500 g / 1 lb 2 oz green
beans

1 tbsp coconut oil, melted

Fine sea salt

Romesco Sauce (recipe
follows)

Romesco is an intensely delicious sauce from the northeastern region
of Spain, where fishermen typically serve it alongside white fish, but
it's delicious with grilled and roasted vegetables, eggs and cooked
grains, and it can even be thinned out a little to make a dressing for
salad leaves. Made with roasted red peppers, almonds, tomato purée,
garlic and smoked paprika, it hits all the umami notes, making the sauce
satisfying, which is not typical of a simple vegetarian dish. I love pairing
it with charred green beans; it's like a far more sophisticated and healthy
version of chips and ketchup that kids will love.

SERVES 4

1 Preheat your grill (or stovetop grill pan) to high.

2 Wash and trim the green beans. Lightly coat them in the coconut oil
and place under the grill. Cook for 4–5 minutes, then turn and cook for a
further 2–3 minutes until tender and nicely charred.

3 Remove the beans from the heat and season with salt. Serve with
Romesco Sauce.

(recipe continues)

ROMESCO SAUCE

MAKES 375 ML / 13 FL OZ

1 Preheat the oven to 200°C / 400°F / Gas mark 6.

2 Wash the peppers and cut them in half. Remove the stems, seeds and ribs, and coat the pieces lightly with coconut oil. Place on a rimmed baking sheet and roast for 25–35 minutes until blistered and blackened in a few places. Remove the roasted peppers from the baking sheet, place them in a bowl and quickly cover it with clingfilm to steam the peppers, which makes the skin very easy to remove. When they are cool enough to handle, peel the peppers and discard the skins.

3 Lower the oven temperature to 160°C / 325°F / Gas mark 3. Place the almonds on a separate rimmed baking sheet and toast for 10–12 minutes, watching them carefully so that they do not burn. Remove from the oven and set them aside to cool.

4 In a food processor, pulse the garlic until very finely chopped. Add the roasted peppers, almonds, paprika, olive oil, salt, parsley, tomato purée and lemon juice and process until the desired consistency is reached – from slightly chunky to smooth. Season with salt.

4 medium red peppers

Coconut oil

70 g / 2½ oz raw, unsalted almonds

1 garlic clove

1 tsp smoked hot paprika (ground chipotle would also work)

2 tbsp cold-pressed olive oil

¼ tsp fine sea salt, plus extra as needed

3 tbsp chopped fresh flat-leaf parsley

2 tbsp tomato purée

1 tsp freshly squeezed lemon juice

SIMPLE MINT PEA DIP

500 g / 1 lb 2 oz fresh or frozen green peas

7 g / ¼ oz fresh mint leaves

1 large garlic clove

2 tbsp tahini

4 tbsp freshly squeezed lemon juice

2 tbsp cold-pressed olive oil

½ tsp fine sea salt

This recipe appeared on my blog some years back, but it's still the preferred snack in my house because it is fast and easy to make. It's both light and rich at the same time, and it pairs well with any spring or early summer veggies, crackers or other 'dippables'. I even like to spread it on a large lettuce or cabbage leaf, wrap it up and munch away. Peas and mint are a classic combo, and the lemon adds gorgeous brightness. Tahini, a slightly unusual addition, grounds everything in its satisfying nuttiness and makes the dip deliciously creamy. You can use fresh, raw peas for this recipe, but blanching them for just a couple of minutes brings out their delicate sweetness and enhances the overall flavour.

SERVES 4–6

1 Fill a small saucepan with water and bring it to the boil. Add the peas and cook for 2–3 minutes until they are bright green and sweet, being careful not to overcook. Drain and rinse the peas under very cold water to halt the cooking process. Set aside.

2 Roughly chop the mint leaves. Set aside.

3 In a food processor, pulse the garlic until very finely chopped. Add the peas, mint, tahini, lemon juice, olive oil and salt, and purée until smooth.

4 Store in an airtight container in the fridge for 3–4 days, but try to consume this dip as quickly as possible.

ROLLOVER Use this pea dip instead of hummus in the Rainbow Hummus Bowl (page 74).

SPICY FRICOS

Get your frico on! Fricos are small rounds of baked cheese that turn miraculously crunchy in the oven, and with just two ingredients, they are probably the simplest snack to make. Though they are typically prepared with Parmesan, in my version I use a hard sheep's milk cheese called Pecorino Romano, which is very similar. If you cannot find Pecorino at your supermarket, use Parmesan instead, but it's important that it comes in a wedge, not pre-grated. Fricos are very tasty served as a nibble before dinner with a crisp, sparkling beverage, or on top of a simple green salad. If you're not into spicy food, simply leave out the crushed chilli flakes for a one-ingredient treat!

75 g / 2¾ oz freshly grated Pecorino Romano

½–1 tsp crushed chilli flakes (depending on how spicy you like them)

MAKES ABOUT 15 CHIPS —————————————

1 Preheat the oven to 160°C / 325°F / Gas mark 3.

2 In a medium bowl, combine the cheese and the chilli flakes, stirring to incorporate.

3 Line a rimmed baking sheet with baking paper. Place heaped tablespoons of the grated cheese and chilli flake mixture about 2.5 cm / 1 in apart on the baking paper and press down lightly with the bottom of a glass to flatten them slightly. Bake for 8–10 minutes until golden. Remove from the oven and leave to cool completely. Store leftovers in an airtight container at room temperature for up to 3 days.

ROLLOVER For extra crunch, use these instead of goat's cheese in the Balsamic-roasted Plums with Spinach and Goat's Cheese (page 70).

ROASTED SESAME AVOCADO CREAM

2 tbsp raw, unsalted sesame seeds

1 garlic clove

Flesh of 2 ripe avocados

4 tbsp freshly squeezed lime juice, plus extra as liked

2 tbsp tahini

¼ tsp pure maple syrup (optional)

Fine sea salt

20 g / ¾ oz fresh coriander leaves

½ sheet of nori, sliced into very thin strips (optional)

Inspired by the Japanese flavour combination of avocado, sesame and nori, I made an avocado dip full of surprises! The tahini adds a satisfying richness and complexity, while the toasted sesame seeds bring on the nuttiness and impart a wonderful contrast to the smooth creaminess. Serve this dip with vegetables or crackers, or use it in a sandwich or lettuce wrap instead of mayonnaise.

SERVES 4

1 Preheat a dry frying pan over a medium heat. When hot, toast the sesame seeds, stirring frequently, until they are fragrant and beginning to pop, 2–3 minutes. Remove the pan from the heat and set aside.

2 In a food processor, pulse the garlic until very finely chopped.

3 Add the avocados, lime juice, tahini, maple syrup, salt and coriander. Purée until smooth and creamy. Taste and adjust the seasoning as needed. Fold in half of the sesame seeds and, if liked, the nori.

4 Spread the dip out on a large plate. Sprinkle with the remaining sesame seeds and, if liked, more nori strips. Serve immediately.

ROLLOVER This is a delicious dip to use with the So-simple Roasted Roots with Dukkah (page 183).

QUINOA CORN MUFFINS

Growing up in the southern United States instilled in me a serious love of cornbread, but the high amounts of butter, cream and sugar in classic versions negate most of the health benefits of the other ingredients. My recipe swaps white flour with cornflour, and sugar with maple syrup, and adds wonderful texture with cooked quinoa. The chilli delivers a swift kick, and the coriander adds tons of southwestern style. These muffins are delicious served alongside a steaming bowl of chilli (page 138) or a black bean salad.

MAKES 12 MUFFINS ————————————————————

1 Preheat the oven to 200°C / 400°F / Gas mark 6. Line a cupcake tin with 12 muffin cases.

2 In a large bowl, sift together the polenta, cornflour, baking powder, bicarbonate of soda and salt. Add the cooked quinoa.

3 In a separate bowl, whisk together the milk, eggs, coconut oil and maple syrup.

4 Add the wet ingredients to the dry and combine in as few strokes as possible. Fold in the coriander and very finely chopped chilli.

5 Spoon the batter into the muffin cases until they are three-quarters full and sprinkle evenly with the pumpkin seeds. Bake for about 25 minutes until the edges are golden brown and a cocktail stick comes out clean when inserted into the middle of a muffin. The muffins are best enjoyed fresh but will keep in an airtight container at room temperature for 3–4 days.

250 g / 9 oz polenta

75 g / 2¾ oz cornflour

1 tbsp baking powder

½ tsp bicarbonate of soda

1 tsp fine sea salt

140 g / 5 oz cooked quinoa (from about 55 g / 2 oz dry)

250 ml / 8 fl oz plant-based milk of your choice

3 large eggs

5 tbsp coconut oil, melted

1½ tsp pure maple syrup

15 g / ½ oz chopped fresh coriander leaves and tender stems

1 small red chilli (stem and seeds removed), very finely chopped (Serrano is a good choice)

3 tbsp raw, unsalted pumpkin seeds

LOGIC-DEFYING COURGETTE FRIES

140 g / 5 oz freshly grated Pecorino Romano (Parmesan will also work)

1 tsp garlic powder

1½ tsp freshly ground black pepper

½ tsp fine sea salt

2 tsp dried oregano

3–4 medium courgettes

1 tbsp coconut oil or ghee, melted

Hot sauce, to serve (optional)

Is it nuts to suggest that you or anyone you know would eat an entire courgette in one sitting? I wager that you'll actually be *fighting* over the last pieces of these totally surprising and, dare I say it, addictive nibbles! Even picky kids I know who claim not to like vegetables gobble them up and beg for more.

The base of cheese, salt and pepper is lovely with the addition of oregano, but rosemary, thyme or crushed chilli flakes also make a tasty change. If your supermarket does not sell Pecorino cheese, a wedge of Parmesan will work.

SERVES 4

1 Preheat the oven to 180°C / 350°F / Gas mark 4. Set a wire rack inside a rimmed baking sheet.

2 In a medium bowl, combine the cheese, garlic powder, black pepper, salt and oregano.

3 Slice the courgette into thin wedges; you should get about 12 pieces from each vegetable. Toss the wedges in the coconut oil to coat, then toss them in the cheese mixture, pressing the wedges into the cheese to set. Place the coated fries on the wire rack.

4 Bake the courgette fries for 12–15 minutes until tender, then place them under the grill for 3–4 minutes until the cheese is golden. Serve immediately with hot sauce, if liked.

ROLLOVER Serve leftover fries with Romesco Sauce (page 195).

CARROT CUMIN FIRECRACKERS

These savoury, spicy crisps are a simple and tasty way to shake up your boxed cracker routine. Never endeavoured to bake crackers before? No worries – these are a cinch to make, and you probably have everything you need in your cupboard right now. The carrots, cumin seeds and crushed chilli flakes really do make these look like pyrotechnic treats, and the taste is simply explosive!

MAKES ABOUT 40 SMALL CRACKERS ──────────────

2 tbsp flaxseeds

180 ml / 6 fl oz water

300 g / 10½ oz gluten-free rolled oats

1 tbsp cumin seeds

½ tsp crushed chilli flakes

½ tsp ground chipotle or smoked hot paprika

1 tsp fine sea salt

3 tbsp coconut oil, melted

1 medium carrot, grated

1 In a small bowl, combine the flaxseeds with half of the water. Set aside to gel, about 15 minutes. Meanwhile, in a food processor, pulse 275 g / 9¾ oz of the oats until they resemble a rough flour. Add the spices and salt; pulse to incorporate.

2 Transfer the oat mixture to a large bowl. Add the coconut oil, flaxseed gel and the remaining water; stir to combine. Add the carrots and finish mixing.

3 Preheat the oven to 180°C / 350°F / Gas mark 4. Divide the dough in half and place one half on a large sheet of baking paper and then set another sheet on top.

4 Using a rolling pin, roll out the dough into a very thin round or square. Remove the top layer of baking paper and sprinkle 2 tablespoons of the remaining rolled oats on top, replace the paper and roll to set.

5 Remove the top piece of baking paper and score the dough into the desired cracker shapes (squares, rectangles, triangles) using the tip of a sharp knife. Slide the dough and the baking paper onto a rimmed baking sheet and place it in the oven.

6 Bake the crackers for 25–30 minutes until fragrant and golden brown. Repeat steps 4 through 6 with the remaining dough.

SOURED CREAM AND ONION
CHICKPEA CRISPS

If you love soured cream 'n' onion chips, you will totally flip over these
salty and super-crunchy chickpea crisps. Pack them in your kids'
lunchboxes, too, or serve them at cocktail hour instead of nuts or crisps.
I always make a double batch so I have extra to garnish salads and soups
with a great gluten-free, high-protein croûton replacement. Keep in
mind that the chickpeas will crisp up quite a bit outside of the oven, so
it's okay if they are still a little soft when they are finished roasting.

3 tbsp coconut oil

1½ tsp freshly squeezed
lemon juice

2 tsp dried dill

4 tsp onion powder

1 tsp fine sea salt

450 g / 1 lb (2 400 g /
14 oz cans) cooked
chickpeas, drained
and rinsed

SERVES 4–6

1 Preheat the oven to 200°C / 400°F / Gas mark 6. In a small saucepan,
melt the coconut oil over a low heat. Whisk in the lemon juice, dill, onion
powder and salt. Remove from the heat and cover to keep warm.

2 Spread the chickpeas out on clean kitchen towel and rub them dry,
discarding any loose skins (the chickpeas will not crisp in the oven if
wet). Place the chickpeas in a large bowl and toss them with the coconut
oil mixture.

3 Spread the chickpeas on a large rimmed baking sheet lined with
baking paper and roast, stirring occasionally, for 25–35 minutes until
golden and crisp.

4 Remove the chickpeas from the oven. Leave them to cool and serve
at room temperature. Store in an airtight glass container at room
temperature for up to 1 week.

ROLLOVER Use these in place of the croûtons in the Grilled Caesar Salad
with Chickpea Croûtons (page 61).

SPICY-SWEET
PUMPKIN SEED SNACKS

At this point in the cookbook, you may be aware of how obsessed I am with salty-sweet combinations. The one-two punch of this flavour coupling strikes a primordial chord that tells our brains we're satisfied, so I try to include a touch of both in almost everything I make. These immensely fulfilling (and addictive) nibbles are the perfect thing to whip up as an alternative to crackers or cookies when I host friends for tea. The maple syrup gives the seeds a hint of sweetness and balances the salty tamari notes and the hit of spice. Try them at cocktail hour instead of fried and sodium-heavy prepared nuts, or snack on them instead of crisps during a film. They also are great sprinkled on top of soup or salad.

2 tsp coconut oil, melted

1 tbsp pure maple syrup

1 tbsp gluten-free tamari or soy sauce

¼ tsp ground cumin

¼ tsp red chilli powder

⅛ tsp smoked hot paprika (ground chipotle would also work)

150 g / 5½ oz raw, unsalted pumpkin seeds

SERVES 4

ROLLOVER These are delicious crumbled on top of the Cashew Corn Chowder with Chipotle Oil (page 38).

1 Preheat the oven to 150°C / 300°F / Gas mark 2. Line a rimmed baking sheet with baking paper.

2 In large mixing bowl, whisk together the coconut oil, maple syrup, tamari, cumin, chilli powder and paprika. Add the pumpkin seeds and stir to coat. Pour the seeds onto the prepared baking sheet, spread them out evenly without too much overlap and place in the oven.

3 After about 10 minutes, remove the seeds from the oven and stir them, again making sure they are evenly spread out. Roast for a further 7–10 minutes, then stir the seeds and spread them out evenly again, this time ensuring that the seeds are touching but not piled on top of one another. Roast for a further 2–3 minutes, then remove from the oven and leave them to cool for at least 15 minutes without disturbing them.

4 When the seeds are cool, lightly break them apart into small portions; they should stick together in free-form, lacy sections. If needed, transfer them to kitchen towel to absorb any excess oil. Store in an airtight container at room temperature for up to 1 week.

SUNBUTTER RYE TOASTS

with Salted Maple Strawberries

400 g / 14 oz raw, unsalted, shelled sunflower seeds

Cold-pressed olive oil (optional)

2 tsp ground cinnamon (optional)

½ tsp fine sea salt (optional)

4 slices wholemeal rye bread

1 batch Salted Maple Strawberries (recipe follows)

ROLLOVER Use the extra sunflower butter and make the Double Chocolate Chunk Sunbutter Cookies (page 228) or as a substitute for the almond butter in Brilliant Banana Almond Soft-serve (page 221).

Living in Denmark has given me a deep appreciation for rye bread. It's not just popular here, it's an everyday staple that you'll see sitting on the work surface like a glorious, malty brown brick, no matter whose home you're in. This recipe is a quick little snack that really satisfies. Homemade sunflower seed butter (or 'sunbutter') is simple to make and a delicious alternative to peanut butter. Here I've paired it with toasted dark rye and strawberries that have been macerated in maple syrup and a little salt to bring out their sweetness. This combo is also delicious on top of yogurt or ice cream, morning oats or even blended into a smoothie, if you have any leftovers.

SERVES 4

1 Preheat the oven to 180°C / 350°F / Gas mark 4.

2 Place the sunflower seeds in an even layer on a rimmed baking sheet and toast for 10–15 minutes until golden and fragrant. Remove them from the oven and leave to cool.

3 Place the cooled sunflower seeds in a food processor and pulse, occasionally scraping down the sides, until smooth and creamy (this process can take 10 minutes or more, so be patient). If the seeds are not releasing their oil, add a little olive oil to help the process along. Once the mixture is creamy, add the cinnamon and sea salt, if using, and blend to incorporate. Store the sunbutter in an airtight glass jar in the fridge for up to 1 month.

4 To assemble, toast the rye bread until dark around the edges. Spread the desired amount of sunbutter over the toast and top with the Salted Maple Strawberries. Serve immediately.

SALTED MAPLE STRAWBERRIES

SERVES 2–4

Hull and quarter the strawberries, and place them in a bowl with the maple syrup and salt. Crush a few berries with a fork on the side of the bowl and stir to mix the juices with the syrup. Leave the strawberries to marinate at room temperature for 5–10 minutes, then enjoy over toast.

(V) (GF) (R) (GrF)

250 g / 9 oz strawberries

1 tbsp pure maple syrup

Pinch of fine sea salt

SWEET POTATO DATE MUFFINS

DRY INGREDIENTS

150 g / 5½ oz wholegrain wheat flour

2 tsp baking powder

½ tsp bicarbonate of soda

2 tsp ground cinnamon

1 tsp ground ginger

¼ tsp fine sea salt

100 g / 3½ oz rolled oats

150 g / 5½ oz chopped dates

WET INGREDIENTS

4 tbsp coconut oil, melted, plus extra for greasing the muffin tin

2 ripe bananas

275 g / 9¾ oz sweet potato purée (from about 1 large roasted sweet potato)

5 tbsp pure maple syrup

2 tsp pure vanilla extract

185 ml / 6½ fl oz plant-based milk of your choice

OPTIONAL ADD-INS

Handful of chopped raw, unsalted pecans

Zest of 1 orange

There is a vegan café in Toronto that serves *the best* muffins, but when a local reporter revealed the nutrition analysis, I – along with everyone who loves them – was completely shocked at how high the fat, salt and calorie contents were. I set out to make a *much* more virtuous version with all the yumminess of the original. Sweet potato purée and banana bind the ingredients together (so you can skip the eggs), while adding a light, natural sweetness to the batter. Studded with juicy dates and rolled oats, these muffins are perfect as a snack when you're on the go or as a light breakfast. Add the optional orange zest and pecans for even more flavour and texture.

MAKES 12 MUFFINS

1 Preheat the oven to 190°C / 375°F / Gas mark 5. Lightly grease a 12-hole muffin tin with coconut oil and set it aside.

2 In a large bowl, sift together the flour, baking powder, bicarbonate of soda, cinnamon, ginger and salt. Add the oats and stir to combine.

3 In a food processor, pulse to combine the bananas, sweet potato purée, maple syrup, coconut oil, vanilla and milk. Pour these wet ingredients over the dry ingredients and stir to combine, using as few strokes as possible. Fold in the chopped dates and optional add-ins.

4 Drop a few tablespoons of the batter into each muffin hole and bake for about 30 minutes until they are golden, fragrant and pass the cocktail stick test. Store leftover muffins in an airtight container in the fridge for up to 5 days, or in the freezer for 1 month.

SPICY WATERMELON MOJITO ICE LOLLIES

Inspired by the popular cocktail, I've taken the classic lime-and-mint combination to the next level. The coolness of the frozen watermelon and mint with a spicy wink of cayenne is surprising and delicious. If you are making these for kids, you can certainly reduce or omit the cayenne, but the adults in your life will undoubtedly appreciate the sophisticated kick in these beauties – like eating fire and ice at the same time!

MAKES 10 ICE LOLLIES

1 Cut the watermelon into chunks, remove the rind and place the flesh in a blender. Blend on medium-low speed until the mixture is liquefied. Strain the juice through a sieve into a jug with a spout and press the pulp to extract as much juice as possible. Discard the pulp.

2 Return the juice to the blender and add the lime juice, cayenne, maple syrup and mint leaves. Blend just enough to chop the mint – do not go too far or you'll change the colour of the juice. Leave the mixture to steep for 10 minutes to infuse the juice with the mint. You should end up with at least 750 ml / 1¼ pints of liquid.

3 Brush a little maple syrup on one side of the remaining mint leaves and press them to the insides of the ice lolly moulds – it helps to use a chopstick. Use 2 or 3 leaves per mould. (This is purely for aesthetics, so if you're pressed for time, skip this step.)

4 Carefully pour a portion of the watermelon juice mixture into each mould, insert the wooden sticks and set the moulds in the freezer for at least 3 hours. To remove the lollies from the moulds, run the moulds under warm water for a few seconds until the lollies release.

1 kg / 2 lb 4 oz seedless watermelon flesh

4 tbsp freshly squeezed lime juice

2 pinches of cayenne, as liked

2 tbsp pure maple syrup or raw honey, plus extra for the moulds

3 tbsp fresh mint leaves, plus extra for the moulds

ROLLOVER The juice alone from this recipe is totally incredible. Leave out the cayenne and add a touch of sparkling water for a refreshing summer drink.

HONEY ALMOND GRANOLA BARS

200 g / 7 oz rolled oats

135 g / 4¾ oz raw, unsalted almonds (hazelnuts, pecans, and walnuts are also delicious here)

2 tbsp coconut oil

125 ml / 4 fl oz raw honey

125 ml / 4 fl oz tahini

1 tsp pure vanilla extract

85 g / 3 oz unsulphured dried fruit (raisins, dates, figs, prunes, apricots or a combination), roughly chopped

55 g / 2 oz puffed whole-grain cereal (such as rice puffs)

¼ tsp sea salt flakes

I grew up with a granola bar in my lunch bag every day, and no matter how old I get, I know I will always love biting into a sweet, gooey, nutty treat. These bars are the perfect on-the-go snack and hopefully will replace the shop-bought varieties, which are often loaded with hidden processed sugars and fats.

It's important to toast the oats and almonds here, as both contain an unwanted compound called phytic acid, which is destroyed by heat. The bonus to this step is gaining heaps of extra flavour from toasting the nuts and grains. Feel free to change the dried fruit: raisins, dates, prunes, cranberries and figs are all tasty options.

MAKES 14 BARS ─────────────────────────────

1 Preheat the oven to 160°C / 325°F / Gas mark 3. Line a brownie tin with clingfilm or baking paper.

2 Place the oats and almonds on a rimmed baking sheet, trying to keep them as separate as possible, and bake, stirring once or twice, for 12–15 minutes until the oats are golden and have a toasted aroma. Remove from the oven, leave to cool and roughly chop the almonds.

3 In a small saucepan, melt the coconut oil over a low heat. Add the honey, tahini and vanilla; whisk until combined. Remove from the heat.

4 In a large bowl, combine the oats and almonds with the dried fruit, puffed cereal and salt. Pour the wet ingredients over the dry and stir quickly.

5 Spoon the mixture into the prepared brownie tin and, using slightly damp hands, press it firmly into the tin, especially around the edges and corners. Set the tin in the fridge for a couple of hours to firm up, then remove and slice into 14 bars. Store the bars in an airtight container in the fridge for up 2 weeks, or wrap them individually for to-go snacks.

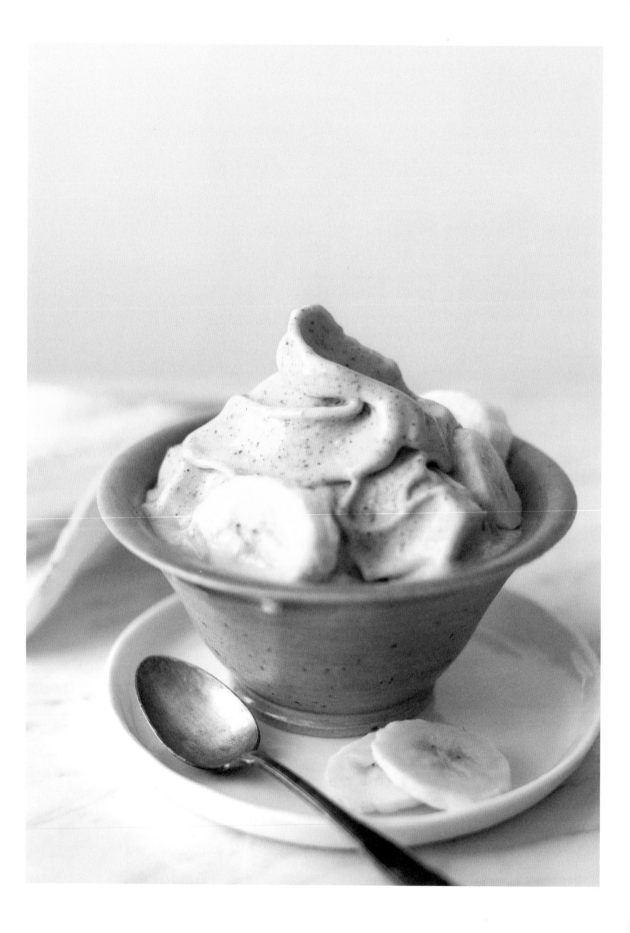

BRILLIANT BANANA ALMOND SOFT-SERVE

If you've had people over for dinner in the last decade, you'll probably be familiar with the challenge of feeding someone with a food intolerance or a lifestyle that doesn't include dairy, eggs, gluten, sugar. . . *whatever*. Well, now you can definitely say that you have dessert covered, because this ice cream checks all the boxes, no matter what the restriction!

Frozen bananas miraculously whip up to make the creamiest, most delicious soft-serve ice cream on their own, but roasted almond butter, vanilla and a little sea salt make this dessert really special. If you or someone you are serving has a nut allergy, feel free to use seed butter (such as sunbutter, page 212) instead of the almond butter, or omit it altogether.

2 ripe bananas

1–2 tbsp almond butter (or your preferred nut/seed butter)

¼ tsp pure vanilla extract

Pinch of fine sea salt

SERVES 1–2

1 Peel the bananas and break them into small chunks. Place them in a sealed plastic bag in the freezer for at least 8 hours.

2 Remove the bananas from the freezer and leave to thaw for 5–10 minutes just slightly. In a food processor, combine the bananas, almond butter, vanilla and salt. Purée until smooth and creamy. Serve immediately.

COCONUT CARDAMOM BLUEBERRY SNACK CAKE

Coconut oil, for greasing the tin

DRY INGREDIENTS

90 g / 3¼ oz unsweetened desiccated coconut, plus a little extra to garnish

100 g / 3½ oz rolled oats

170 g / 6 oz wholemeal flour

1½ tsp baking powder

½ tsp bicarbonate of soda

1–2 tsp ground cardamom (depending on your preference)

¾ tsp fine sea salt

WET INGREDIENTS

1 400 ml / 14 fl oz can full-fat coconut milk

Zest of 1 lemon

2 tbsp freshly squeezed lemon juice

2 tsp pure vanilla extract

4 tbsp pure maple syrup

2 large eggs

115 g / 4 oz blueberries, fresh or thawed frozen

There are two kinds of people in this world: those who like icing and those who do not. I fall into the latter camp and was one of those freaky kids who scraped the thick layer of sugar-schmear off her birthday cake and gave it to her best friend. Now that you know this about me, you'll understand my motivation for making this snack cake. Because there is no icing, it is easily portable and hand-held. I dialled down the sweetness that you would normally find in a dessert cake, so keep that in mind when you're enjoying it. The benefit of this is that you can definitely eat this cake for breakfast! Who can argue with that?

MAKES 16 PIECES

1 Preheat the oven to 180°C / 350°F / Gas mark 4. Lightly grease a 20 × 20 cm / 8 × 8 in brownie tin with coconut oil.

2 In a large bowl, combine the dry ingredients: the coconut, oats, flour, baking powder, bicarbonate of soda, cardamom and salt.

3 In a medium bowl, whisk together the wet ingredients: the coconut milk, lemon zest and juice, vanilla, maple syrup and eggs. Pour the wet ingredients over the dry ingredients and stir to combine in as few strokes as possible. Fold in the blueberries. Pour the batter into the prepared tin. Sprinkle with the remaining coconut.

4 Bake for 35–40 minutes until a cocktail stick comes out clean when inserted into the middle of the cake. Leave the cake to cool completely, then slice it into 16 squares. Store in an airtight container in the fridge for up to 5 days.

TOASTED WALNUT BROWNIE BITES, 3 WAYS

One of the most successful recipes on my blog is undoubtedly the Raw Brownie. With its super-short ingredient list, foolproof method and wildly delicious results, it's no wonder that so many people have opened their mind to healthier sweets because of it. If you want to keep the base recipe as it is, be my guest! But I've given you three other options to suit a number of tastes. If you're making these for a buffet or party, for instance, it's fun to offer a few variations.

Store the brownies in the freezer until you're ready to serve them. Although delicious at room temperature, they are also really good cold.

BROWNIE DOUGH

MAKES 500 G / 1 LB 2 OZ DOUGH

130 g / 4½ oz raw, unsalted walnuts

70 g / 2½ oz cocoa powder

¼ tsp fine sea salt

300 g / 10½ oz soft dates (preferably Medjool)

1 Preheat the oven to 180°C / 350°F / Gas mark 4.

2 Place the walnuts on a rimmed baking sheet and toast for 7–10 minutes until they are lightly coloured and fragrant. Remove from the oven and leave them to cool.

3 In a food processor, pulse the walnuts until they are finely ground. Add the cocoa and salt. Pulse to combine.

4 Stone the dates and add them one at a time through the feed tube of the food processor while it is running. You should end up with a mixture that resembles cake crumbs but, when pressed, will easily stick together (if the mixture does not hold together well, add more dates).

5 Use the dough to make the Brownie Bites that follow. Leftover dough will keep in the freezer for up to 1 month.

ESPRESSO BROWNIE BITES

MAKES ABOUT 10 BALLS ————————————————————

Combine the dough with the espresso powder, using your hands to fully incorporate the ingredients. Shape the dough into 10 small bite-sized balls. Freeze the balls until ready to eat. Store in the freezer for up to 1 month.

⅓ batch (about 165 g / 5¾ oz) of Brownie Dough (page 224)

¾ tsp espresso powder

VANILLA COCONUT BROWNIE BITES

MAKES ABOUT 10 BALLS ————————————————————

Combine the dough with the vanilla and 1½ teaspoons of the coconut, using your hands to fully incorporate the ingredients. Shape the dough into 10 small bite-sized balls, then roll them in the remaining coconut. Freeze the balls until ready to eat. Store in the freezer for up to 1 month.

⅓ batch (about 165 g / 5¾ oz) of Brownie Dough (page 224)

1 tsp pure vanilla extract

3 tbsp unsweetened desiccated coconut, toasted

SPICED ORANGE BROWNIE BITES

MAKES ABOUT 10 BALLS ————————————————————

Combine the dough with the orange zest, cinnamon and cayenne, if liked, using your hands to fully incorporate the ingredients. Shape the dough into 10 small bite-sized balls. Freeze the balls until ready to eat. Store in the freezer for up to 1 month.

⅓ batch (about 165 g / 5¾ oz) of Brownie Dough (page 224)

Zest of 1 orange

¼ tsp ground cinnamon

Pinch of cayenne (optional)

DOUBLE CHOCOLATE CHUNK
SUNBUTTER COOKIES

2 large eggs

2 tsp pure vanilla extract

250 g / 9 oz sunbutter
(page 212)

125 ml / 4 fl oz pure maple
syrup

1 tsp bicarbonate of soda

¼ tsp fine sea salt

45 g / 1½ oz cocoa powder

100 g / 3½ oz dark
chocolate (70% or higher),
roughly chopped

170 g / 6 oz raw, unsalted,
shelled sunflower seeds

I'm pretty convinced that whatever your question might be, these cookies are the answer. They are miraculously made without a speck of flour, instead using sunflower seed butter as their base, which yields a super rich, moist and satisfying result. They are surprisingly cakey and unapologetically fudgey with their dark chocolate chunks (not chips – a crucial distinction). The sunflower seed coating around the outside adds a wicked crunch and textural balance to the chewiness, but you could use another type of seed or nut if you like – chopped hazelnuts would be divine.

MAKES 20 COOKIES

1 Preheat the oven to 160°C / 325°F / Gas mark 3. Line a rimmed baking sheet with baking paper.

2 In a small bowl, whisk together the eggs and vanilla. Add the sunbutter and mix thoroughly. Add the maple syrup, bicarbonate of soda and salt and fold together. Sift in the cocoa powder and stir to incorporate. Fold in the chopped chocolate.

3 Place the sunflower seeds in a separate bowl. Wet your hands slightly with water. Divide the dough into about 20 portions and roll each into a rough ball (the dough will be very wet, but this is normal!).

4 Drop the dough balls into the bowl of seeds and roll to coat them in the seeds. Flatten the balls out slightly and place them on the prepared baking sheet about 5 cm / 2 in apart.

5 Bake the cookies for 10–13 minutes until they have risen and expanded. Leave them to cool slightly before serving. Store the cookies in an airtight container at room temperature for up to 1 week.

BUYING AND STORING KITCHEN STAPLES

The following ingredients are what I would consider kitchen staples, and for that reason it's important to invest in good-quality versions of them. If you can't get some of these things at your local shop, I think they are worth a trip to the health food store (or order them online), since you will be using them very frequently.

Cold-pressed Olive Oil
Buying: When purchasing olive oil, look for a product in a dark glass bottle. Light destroys the delicate nutrients in the oil, so it's essential that the coloured glass is green, brown or blue, not clear. Never purchase olive oil in a plastic container. It's okay to purchase oil sold in a tin, but be sure to transfer it to a dark glass bottle when you get home. Look for the terms *unrefined* and *cold-pressed* on the label, meaning that it was extracted on the first pressing, processed at lower temperatures without chemicals, and still contains the most nutrition and flavour.

Storing: Olive oil will keep for 2–3 months after opening, so buy only the amount you need and use it up before then. Store it away from heat: in the fridge or in a very small bottle in a relatively cool, dark place.

Coconut Oil
Burnt and oxidized fats cause free-radical damage in the body (that means no more cooking with olive oil!), so it's important to cook with oils that have a high smoke point. Coconut oil is a great choice.

Buying: To avoid coconut's overwhelming flavour, choose expeller-pressed, steam-refined, non-hydrogenated coconut oil, which has a neutral taste. Cold-pressed virgin coconut oil has a strong flavour and is best with raw foods.

Storing: Because it is so stable, coconut oil can be stored at room temperature for up to 1 year. If coconut oil comes packaged in plastic, transfer it to a glass jar.

Soy Sauce and Tamari
Soy sauce comes in two varieties: light and dark. The light one is lighter in colour with a low viscosity and is extremely salty. This type is more expensive than the dark and is used as a condiment at the table. Dark soy sauce is deep in colour with a higher viscosity and a sweeter flavour (usually due to additives such as caramel colour or molasses). Dark soy sauce is used more frequently in cooking. Tamari is my top pick for soy-based sauces, because it is gluten-free (check the label – it must say gluten- and wheat-free). Tamari is traditionally brewed, has a stronger flavour than soy sauce and is best used to season longer-cooking foods, such as soups, stews and baked dishes.

Buying: I highly recommend purchasing good-quality soy products whenever possible. Look for the terms *traditionally brewed*, *organic* and *non-GMO*. The conventional and less expensive versions of this seasoning may contain food dyes, refined sweeteners, preservatives and chemical residues from processing.

Storing: Opened soy condiments will keep in the fridge for 2–3 months.

Fine and Salt Flakes
There are two types of salt I use on a daily basis: fine and sea salt flakes. Fine sea salt is good for seasoning during cooking and, of course, baking, because it is easy to measure and dissolves evenly. Sea salt flakes have a coarse texture that makes it easy to pinch between your fingers and sprinkle onto cooked foods as a garnish or to adjust the seasoning. Avoid table salt – it is highly refined with many additives and

has an unpleasant, bitter aftertaste that can spoil the delicate flavours of food (plus, after processing, table salt can be just as harmful as processed white sugar – although it is generally eaten in much smaller quantities).

Buying: When purchasing salt, look for all-natural, dried (not boiled), unrefined salts with no added ingredients. Sea salt and Himalayan crystal salt are the types I use most often.

Storing: Store salt in glass, ceramic, stone or wood containers (do not store it in metal, or it will corrode the container), or keep small amounts in a salt cellar on your work surface for easy access. Salt will keep indefinitely if stored in a dry, clean environment.

Black Pepper

Black pepper does not have to be expensive, but I do insist that it is ground fresh in a pepper mill.

Buying: Always purchase whole black peppercorns. For my recipes, I like a medium-coarse grind from a pepper mill. Invest in a good mill, grind your own and your life will be forever changed.

Storing: Store whole black peppercorns as you would all spices, in an airtight container away from heat and light. Peppercorns will keep for 1–2 years.

Lemon

When a recipe in this book calls for lemon juice, I am referring to freshly squeezed lemon juice from the real citrus fruit, not the liquid in a yellow plastic lemon (which contains preservatives and sulphites).

Buying: I call for lemon zest quite often in this book – it has a ton of flavour! For this reason, try to buy organic lemons if you can find them. But if you can only find conventional lemons, wash them really well.

Storing: Lemons kept in an airtight bag in the fridge will stay juicy and fresh for up to 1 month.

Apple Cider Vinegar

Apple cider vinegar adds delicious zing to all kinds of foods and is perfect for pickling. It is rich in enzymes, aids digestion, alkalinizes the body and supports a healthy immune system – truly a miracle food!

Buying: Made from fermented apple cider, apple cider vinegar should always be purchased

SHOPPING REMINDERS

The supermarket can be an overwhelming place, especially if you are trying to make healthier choices. Keep these tips in mind on your next trip to the shops.

Stick to the outside. The perimeter of every supermarket is where you'll find the freshest things: fruits, vegetables, bread, eggs and dairy, with produce typically situated right near the front door. This is where you'll want to spend the bulk of your time (and budget). Lastly, take a quick trip to the centre aisles to grab dried staples such as grains, beans and spices. If your shop has bulk bins, use them! Buying dried goods in bulk, instead of in packets, is often far less expensive.

Read labels. In general, only purchase things with one ingredient ('chickpeas', or 'almonds', for example). If you are buying packaged items, watch for terms that are vague and misleading: *all natural, fresh, healthy, wholegrain, diet, light, no added sugar, fortified, enriched, low-fat* and *fat-free.* Even packaged food labelled as organic should be scrutinized, because such a label refers to the agricultural process, not the food's health properties. Just because the food is organic doesn't necessarily mean it's good for you – white sugar can be made organically too!

Make a list. Writing down and sticking to a shopping list will help save you time, money and energy in the shop. Try to keep your impulse buys to the produce aisle.

unpasteurized (raw), unfiltered with 'the mother' (the cobweb-like strands of good bacteria in the vinegar), and organic, if possible. Look for it in glass bottles.

Storing: Apple cider vinegar is highly acidic, so it can last for many months outside of the fridge without spoiling, but keeping it in a cool, dry place away from direct sunlight, such as in a store cupboard, is still important. If you know that you won't be using it very often, I suggest keeping it in the fridge.

Pure Maple Syrup

Maple syrup is by far my favourite sweetener, conveniently gluten-free, vegan and easy to find.

It's true that it may be more expensive than other sweeteners, but I believe it is worth the investment for both taste and nutrition.

Buying: When purchasing maple syrup, it's essential to read the ingredients list – it should have only 100 per cent pure maple syrup listed. Avoid buying a product that contains maple flavour, high-fructose corn syrup or other sweeteners, or that is labelled with the term *pancake syrup*. If your supermarket offers different grades of maple syrup, choose Grade B over Grade A. Grade B maple syrup is from sap that is collected later in the season, is deeper in colour, far more flavourful and contains higher amounts of minerals.

Storing: Open bottles of pure maple syrup should be stored in the fridge and will keep for up to 1 year.

Herbs

Fresh herbs are not just a garnish in my recipes; they are a critical element that can take a weeknight meal to great heights and help transform a humble pot of brown rice into something special. Most people's main complaint about herbs is that they buy a bunch for a teaspoon or so to use in one recipe and the rest of it rots in the fridge! I hope the recipes and Rollover ideas in this book give you plenty of ideas and reasons to use every last scrap of your fresh herbs.

Buying: Purchase fresh herbs that look perky and vibrant, without any signs of discoloration, bruising, mould or slime.

Storing: It's *essential* that you wash your herbs as soon as you get them home from the shop, as dirt, debris and bacteria will cause them to decay more rapidly. I fill my salad spinner with just enough water to cover the herb. Holding the stems, I dunk the herbs up and down into the water several times – as the dirt and debris run off, the water may change colour. If the water is very murky, I repeat until it is clear, then drain the bowl and gently spin the herbs dry.

For tender herbs like coriander, dill, mint and flat-leaf parsley, cut off the ends as you would with flowers, place them in a glass with about 2.5cm / 1 in of water in the bottom, and cover them with a plastic bag, sealing it as tightly as possible at the bottom with a rubber band. Stored this way, tender herbs should keep for 2–3 weeks in the fridge. The only exception is basil, which should be stored at room temperature without a bag over the top.

Wrap washed, sturdy herbs like rosemary, thyme and sage in kitchen paper and place them in a resealable plastic bag in the fridge. Sturdy herbs should keep for 2–3 weeks this way.

Flour

There aren't many recipes in this book that use flour, but the ones that do call for 100 per cent wholegrain, wholemeal flour. If your supermarket sells other wholegrain flours, such as spelt, I always recommend using that over wholemeal.

Buying: The biggest indicator of a good-quality flour is that it has an expiration date listed on the packet. Remember: Real food goes bad! Look for *100 per cent wholegrain* flour from a grain such as wheat.

Storing: Because flour actually expires and turns rancid, it is extremely important to store wholegrain flour in an airtight canister in a cool, dry place. Store it in the freezer if you use it only occasionally.

Bread

Having a loaf of quality bread stashed in your freezer can be a lifesaver when you need to make a satisfying meal or snack in a pinch. Keep one or two varieties on hand, like a dark rye and/or a grainy country-style loaf.

Buying: Fresh is best! The first ingredient in high-quality bread should be 100 per cent wholegrain, wholemeal (or other grain). I always recommend a sourdough loaf instead of one leavened with yeast, because it's far easier to digest and stays fresher about three times as long. Bonus points for finding a bread with sprouted grains, legumes, nuts or seeds in it!

Storing: Bread will keep in an airtight bag at room temperature for about 3 days (any longer and you can bet it has preservatives in it). I like to slice my bread and store it in the freezer. This way, I can take out as many slices as I need at a time and let them thaw at room temperature or put them directly into the toaster. Frozen bread will keep for 6 months if tightly wrapped and sealed. Bread will get stale far faster in the fridge than at room temperature, so avoid storing it in the fridge.

ACKNOWLEDGEMENTS

My name may be the one on the cover, but there are so many people whose energies and spirits played a major role in bringing this book to life.

First, to my husband, Mikkel, for taking the journey with me again. I feel so lucky that we have had the opportunity to truly collaborate on this, because your brilliant ideas, your ability to make sense of my nonsense and your puns make everything so much better. I love you almost as much as tahini. Really close.

To my little star, Finn, for taste testing your way through the book with me and giving me *very* clear feedback. I hope you're not turned off chillies, lemons or raw garlic for the rest of your life. My heart bursts when you beg for more lentils and the fact that you could identify almost every single piece of produce at the supermarket before you could say your own name makes Mama so proud.

To my family, Sheila, Paul, Diana, Trevor and Ali, for agreeing to surf this wave with me once again. Thank you for your patience, encouragement and belief in my dreams. I feel as if I can hear you cheering across the ocean every time I nail another recipe and take another photo that captures how delicious it is. And a special thanks to my mum for grocery shopping, chopping, cooking and cleaning right alongside me. I love you all so much.

To the incredibly generous hands and souls who lovingly donated their precious days to help me in the kitchen: Signe Ågård Christensen, Mia Signe Kähler Albek, Mere Rosenbluth and Gertrud Sol. Your energy was outrageous, contagious and made each day more fun than it should have been. I love that your enthusiasm matched mine so we could celebrate the true joys of sharing food. What a gift you all are.

To Samantha, who has constantly supported and believed in me for so many years now. Look what we have done together! Thank you for creating a space for me to share my passions with the world and for always being on my side.

To my editors, Rica Allannic and Angelin Borsics, for constantly pushing me to think bigger, better and beyond. Your patience, open-mindedness and meticulousness really make this book shine. And to the rest of the Clarkson Potter team for all of your hard work, including Terry Deal, Heather Williamson, La Tricia Watford, Natasha Martin and Stephanie Davis.

To Sharon Bowers, who took the mystery and pressure out of this whole process. You always find a way to make me see the big picture and give me permission to be a human who doesn't always know the answer. Your guidance, support and professionalism mean the world to me.

To Rune Lundø, for once again bringing the best out of my images. I have so much fun learning from you, and I bow to your genius.

To Per Bo, for inspiring me with your beautiful ceramic works and for loaning many of the pieces shown in the book. You are a true artist and friend.

To my incredible recipe testers, who worked so hard and shared your thoughtful feedback with me. Your sincerity and critical assessments helped shape the recipes to be the best they can be. I am eternally grateful to you all: Bettina Abaou, Neeza Adenan, Amal Alhaag, Liz Ball, Renee Barker, Sheila Britton, Stephanie Bonic, Laura Chimelski, Kathryn Coatsworth, Signy Coatsworth, Michelle Cossar, Michele Delios, Anastasia Doudakis, Jenneke Dubois, Kelly Ekardt, Rickard Engstrom, Paula Hannon, Jules Hau, Brigitte Hendrix, Ngoc Hoang, Sharman Howes, Barbara Jacops, Gina Johnston, Kaitlin Kazmierowski, Renee Kemps, Alicia Key, Julie Leach, Debbie Levy, Kristine Lye, Jane Matthews, Shane Mazandarani, Kelly McCabe, Lisa Muller, Adrienne Murphy, Steph Nambiar, Jennifer Northrup, Valerie Orviss, Kinga Pulcinska, Mere Rosenbluth, Natasha Staddon, Ambar Surastri, Jaime Tan, Myra Tay, Misla Tesfamariam, Linda van der Heijden, Alison and Lexie Von Hahn, Aga Wala and Ali Wylie.

And to all of the *My New Roots* readers, your love humbles me to no end. Your willingness to embrace new things and strive towards a healthier life has helped shape and define my purpose in this life. Without you, this cookbook would not exist, and I would get up in the morning to make breakfast just for myself, instead of the hundreds of thousands of you who care to see what I put on top of my smoothie bowl. I am so grateful to be a part of this community.

INDEX